Diet recommendations for gluten sensitive enteropathy

Please check these recommendations always with a nutrition consultant, therapist, doctor or dietician. The recipes and the list of ingredients are supporting the conventional medical therapy.
The calorie disclosures of fresh ingredients (fruit and vegetables) vary according to quality and time of harvest. The contents were checked by a dietician and a nutrition consultant for the Traditional Chinese Medicine (TCM).

Author:
©2017 Josef Miligui
www.ebns.at

AF220868

Source:
The lists are created from the EBNS database for nutritional counseling. The database is used by dietitians, therapists and doctors for advising the patient / client.

Literature:
The specialist literature and the training documents of the German and Austrian dietary and traditional Chinese medicine serve as a knowledge base. We have used the documents as a basis of knowledge, adapted it to our experience and completed them.
http://di-book.com

Title Photo:
©2008 Erika Weixlbaumer

Production and publishing:
BoD – Books on Demand, Norderstedt
ISBN: 9783752889239

Diet recommendations for DIETETICS - Gastrointestinal tract - Small intestine and large intestine - Gluten sensitive enteropathy (celiac disease)

1   Treatment strategy

As an alternative to the gluten-containing grains are expressly allowed:
Millet, corn, rice, amaranth, tapioca, buckwheat, quinoa, soybeans,
chestnut, cooking banana.
Vegetables are allowed including potatoes, salads, fruits, meat and fish,
eggs, milk and dairy products.

2   Avoid

Currently, the only safe way to treat the disease is a lifelong gluten-free
diet, which helps the intestinal mucosa to recover and also reduce the
risks of long-term sequelae (eg colorectal cancer).
Strictly avoid all grain varieties with high gluten content (wheat, barley,
rye, as well as their botanically related origin: spelled, green core,
Emmer and the rye-wheat cross Triticale).
So far, the oats have also been abandoned, although the chemical
composition of the prolamines differs from that of wheat and oats are
released in moderate quantities and under medical supervision for
adults with celiac disease in Finland and England.
Wild rice is now approved for celiac diet.
Particularly when processed foods and finished products are taken,
care must be taken that no gluten-containing ingredients have been
used.
Since gluten is used technologically as an emulsifier, for gelling,
stabilizing and as a carrier of aromatics, this is not always apparent at
first glance.

3   Breakfast

	kkal. per serving
Apple - banana cream	110
Avocado with lemon	289
Banana Soymilk	125
Beef broth	124
Blueberry puree	10

4   Snack

5   Lunch

6 Afternoon

7 Dinner

8 Any time

9 Recipes

(recommendable) = You can use more.
(little) = You should use less than specified or omit.

9.1 Antipasti

Improves blood circulation, anti-inflammatory, relieves pain. Diuretic, promotes digestion, reduces blood pressure. antioxidativ, antibacterial, affects anorexia, improves digestion, flatulence, stomach weakness, stimulating.
Cooking time approx. 40 min
3 portions
Allergens:

Quantity of ingredients
Pepperoni 1 piece / 5g. (yes)
Lemon juice 1 table spoon / 10g. (yes)
Aubergine 1 piece / 300g. (yes)
Tomato 4 pieces / 200g. (recommended)
Zucchini 5/8 oz / 200g. (recommended)
Lemon peel 1/2 piece / 3g. (yes)
Olive oil 1 table spoon / 15g. (yes)
Basil (fresh) 8 leaves / 5g. (yes)
Salt 1 pinch / 0,5g. (little)
Coriander 1/2 teaspoon / 2g. (yes)

Cooking instructions:
Preheat the oven to 250 degrees Celsius and bake the hot peppers until the bowl becomes dark (about 20 minutes). Cover the hot peppers with a clear film and allow to cool. Peel the skin and cut into strips about 2 cm wide. Cut tomatoes in half and spread with oil in slices of aubergine and bake in the oven at 200 degrees golden brown (about 10 minutes) Fry the zucchini slices in the grill pan (without fat).
Mix everything together, mix the marinade of olive oil, salt and lemon peel and pour over the vegetables, sprinkle with coriander. Leave for 1 hour.

9.2 Apple - banana cream

Regulates gastrointestinal function, provides vitamin C, cholesterol lowering, reduces inflammation, diuretic, improves blood circulation.
Cooking time approx. 15 min
Calories p. portion: 110
4 portions
Allergens:

Quantity of ingredients
Apple (sour) 7/8 lbs / 400g. (recommended)
Water 3/4 cup - 6 oz / 200g. (yes)
Orange peel 1/4 piece / 5g. (yes)
Lemon peel 1/2 piece / 2g. (yes)
Sugar brown 2 teaspoons / 6g. (little)
Cinnamon sticks 1 piece / 0g. (yes)
Banana 1 piece / 150g. (yes)
Acerola fruit nectar or powder 1 teaspoon / 2g. (yes)
Orange juice 1/2 piece / 50g. (yes)
Lemon juice 1 table spoon / 10g. (yes)

Cooking instructions:
Cut the apple into fine slices, bring water to boil and add the apple slices, orange- and lemon peel, sugar and cinnamon and simmer about 7 minutes. The apples should be almost soft. Remove acerola and the cinnamon stick.
Mix the apple, the banana, the orange juice and the lemon juice.

9.3 Artichoke soup

Detoxifying, supports urination, regulates digestion, stimulates appetite, gentle laxative, forcing spleen, promotes weight loss. Strengthens gastrointestinal function, expands blood vessels, prevents cancer.
Cooking time approx. 40 min
Calories p. portion: 142
3 portions
Allergens: GLN

Quantity of ingredients
Artichoke 4 pieces / 400g. (yes)
Butter organic 1 table spoon / 20g. (yes)
Onion (shallot) 1 piece / 20g. (yes)
Corn flour 1 table spoon / 10g. (little)

Nutmeg 1 pinch / 0,5g. (yes)
Basic recipe for a vegetable soup (nutritious) 1 cup / 250g. (yes)
Salt 1 pinch / 0,5g. (little)
Lemon 1/4 piece / 8g. (yes)
Lemon peel 1/4 piece / g. (yes)
Turmeric (yellow root) 1 pinch / 1g. (yes)
Sesame paste (Tahini) 1 table spoon / 10g. (yes)
Sesame, white 1 teaspoon / 10g. (little)

Cooking instructions:
Boil the artichokes in 2 liters of water with salt until the outer leaves are light removable. Remove leaves and flower center (fibrous) so that only the soil remains.
Melt the butter, cut the onion into small pieces and steam gently; add some cornmeal, nutmeg; brew with vegetable soup; add salt, a little lemon peel and juice, turmeric and artichoke bottoms, cook gently and puree; Season with Tahin and sprinkle with sesame before serving.

9.4   Asparagus and herb ragout

Diuretic, improves blood circulation, prevents cancer, dissolves stagnation, promotes weight loss. Good to fight immunodeficiency, loss of appetite, flatulence, high blood pressure, depressions, diabetes, diarrhea, stimulates liver function.
Cooking time approx. 30 min
Calories p. portion: 168
4 portions
Allergens: GL

Quantity of ingredients
Basic recipe for a vegetable soup (nutritious) 2 cups / 500g. (yes)
Lemon peel 1/2 piece / 3g. (yes)
Coriander 1/4 teaspoon / 1g. (yes)
Nutmeg 1 pinch / 0,3g. (yes)
Asparagus (green or white) 1,8 lbs / 800g. (recommended)
Parsley 1 Bunch / 125g. (yes)
Créme fraiche cheese 2 table spoons / 30g. (yes)
Lemon juice 1 teaspoon / 3g. (yes)
Potato 7/8 lbs / 400g. (yes)

Cooking instructions:
Cook potatoes with plenty of salted water about 20 min. until soft.
Heat the vegetable stock with lemon zest, coriander and nutmeg till it
boil. Cook the peeled and sliced asparagus in it.
Drain asparagus in a sieve. Collect the cooking liquid.
In the blender mix 200 g of cooked asparagus (the lower ends), cooking
liquid and parsley to a smooth sauce. Beat the sauce with crème fraiche
until smooth. Add asparagus and heat again and season with lemon
juice, salt and pepper. Serve with the potatoes.

9.5 Avocado with lemon

Good to fight insomnia, inflammation, swelling, pain and itching. Is
calming.
Cooking time approx. 5 min
Calories p. portion: 289
1 portions
Allergens:

Quantity of ingredients
Avocado 1/2 piece / 120g. (yes)
Lemon juice 1/2 piece / 10g. (yes)
Salt 1 pinch / 1g. (little)

Cooking instructions:
Halve the avocado, remove the core, add the lemon juice, salt a little
and eat with a spoon.

9.6 Banana Soymilk

Good to fight loss of appetite, oral mucosa inflammation. Strengthens
body energy, promotes stomach-spleen harmony, promotes digestion,
regulates gastrointestinal function, detoxifying, bactericide.
Cooking time approx. 5 min
Calories p. portion: 126
2 portions
Allergens: E

Quantity of ingredients
Banana 1 piece / 120g. (yes)
Soybean milk 1 1/2 cups / 400g. (yes)
Honey 1 teaspoon / 3g. (yes)
Cinnamon ground 1 pinch / 1g. (yes)
Acerola fruit nectar or powder 1 teaspoon / 2g. (yes)

Cooking instructions:
Cut the banana into pieces, puree them with soy milk, acerola, honey and cinnamon with the mixing stick.

9.7   Basic recipe for a beef broth (clear)

Strengthens muscles, tendons and bones, reduces blood pressure, strengthens immune system, prevents cancer, reduces radiation damage, stimulates digestion, reduces pain, promotes digestion, diuretic. Rosemary stimulates digestion.
Cooking time approx. 4-8 hours
Calories p. portion: 114
10 portions
Allergens: O

Quantity of ingredients
Beef soup meat 1,1 lbs / 500g. (yes)
Beef meatbones 5/8 oz / 200g. (yes)
Vinegar (Red wine vinegar) 1 dash / 3g. (yes)
Juniper berry 8 pieces / 6g. (recommended)
Rosemary 1 pinch / 1g. (yes)
Carrot 3 pieces / 210g. (recommended)
Parsnip 2 pieces / 300g. (yes)
Leek 1 piece / 200g. (yes)
Ginger fresh 1/2 teaspoon / 5g. (yes)
Lovage 1 stem / 15g. (yes)
Clove 2 pieces / 2g. (yes)
Pimento 6 pieces / 12g. (yes)
Anise (Common Fennel) 2 pieces / 1g. (yes)
Salt 1 teaspoon / 5g. (little)
Water 3,3 lbs / 1300g. (yes)

Cooking instructions:
Heat water, a dash of red wine vinegar, some juniper berries, a little rosemary, bones and meat till it boils; add carrot, parsnip, leek, ginger, lovage, clove, allspice, star anise and a little salt; simmer for 4-8 hours then strain.
Refrigerate for later use.

9.8 Basic recipe for a chicken broth worming

Strengthens blood, strengthens bone marrow, reduces blood pressure, strengthens immune system, prevents cancer, reduces radiation damage, promotes sweating, dissolves stagnation, good to fight loss of appetite, flatulence.
Cooking time approx. 2-3 hours
Calories p. portion: 90
9 portions
Allergens: L

Quantity of ingredients
Chicken meat 1/2 piece / 600g. (yes)
Carrot 2 pieces / 150g. (recommended)
Leek 1 stick / 45g. (yes)
Celery root 1 piece / 500g. (recommended)
Ginger fresh 2 slices / 2g. (yes)
Fenugreek (Trigonella foenum-graecum) 1 teaspoon / 2g. (yes)
Juniper berry 1 teaspoon / 3g. (recommended)
Bay leaf 3 pieces / 2g. (yes)
Water 4 cup / 900g. (yes)

Cooking instructions:
Remove chicken parts from fat. Place chicken pieces in a saucepan with hot water and heat till it boils briefly, skimming any resulting foam. Add coarsely chopped vegetables and all spices and cook over medium heat for 2 to 3 hours. Strain the finished soup. Throw away vegetables and bones.
Tip: If you want to use the meat as a soup insert, take out after 45 minutes and return only the bones in the soup.
Refrigerate for later use.

9.9 Basic recipe for a duck broth

Forcing spleen, strengthens blood, supports urination, reduces blood pressure, strengthens immune system, prevents cancer, reduces radiation damage.
Cooking time approx. 2-3 hours
Calories p. portion: 61
6 portions
Allergens: L

Quantity of ingredients
Water 2 cup / 450g. (yes)
Duck (heart) 5/8 oz / 200g. (yes)
Duck (slaughtered) 1/4 lbs - 4oz / 100g. (yes)
Carrot 2 pieces / 100g. (recommended)
Celery root 1/2 piece / 600g. (recommended)

Cooking instructions:
Cook duck pieces with vegetables for 2-3 hours. Sift broth through a fine sieve and refrigerate for later use.
The innards can be reused: You cut them finely and leaves them for a few minutes with fresh vegetables in the broth draw. Sprinkle with parsley before serving.

9.10 Basic recipe for a fish broth

Strengthens the kidneys, promotes watering, reduces blood pressure, strengthens immune system, prevents cancer, reduces radiation damage. Low in cholesterol and protein rich, stimulates appetite.
Cooking time approx. 40 min
Calories p. portion: 128
5 portions
Allergens: DLO

Quantity of ingredients
Fish pieces mixed (fresh water) 3/4 lbs / 300g. (recommended)
Celery root 1/4 lbs - 4oz / 120g. (recommended)
Leek 2 inches / 10g. (yes)
Carrot 2 pieces / 150g. (recommended)
White wine 1/2 cup / 125g. (little)
Lemon 1/2 piece / 50g. (yes)
Bay leaf 2 leaves / 2g. (yes)
Peppercorns 3 pieces / 2g. (yes)
Olive oil 1 table spoon / 10g. (yes)
Water 2 cup / 450g. (yes)

Cooking instructions:
Fry celery, chopped carrots and leeks in olive oil, add bay leaf and peppercorns, add pieces of fish and sauté briefly. Add water, add little white wine or lemon. Simmer gently for 30 minutes. Skim off the resulting foam several times. In the end, sift the ingredients through a cloth.
Refrigerate for later use

9.11 Basic recipe for a reissue soup (Congee)

Low fat content, for the drainage of the body overweight and high blood pressure.
Cooking time approx. 2-4 hours
Calories p. portion: 140
3 portions
Allergens:

Quantity of ingredients
Rice variety any 1 cup / 120g. (yes)
Water 6 cups / 700g. (yes)

Cooking instructions:
Cook rice and water in a ratio of about 1: 6. The amount of water determines the thickness of the mash (matter of taste).
Put the rice in a saucepan with a heavy lid. It is important to simmer the rice after a short boil on the slightest flame, otherwise it burns.
Boil the rice for 2-4 hours. The longer he cooks, the more he strengthens.
If you want to eat the dish for breakfast, you can put the rice on just before bedtime.
To be on the safe side, you should first check the behavior of your pot and cooker under observation for a similar amount of time, so that nothing burns.
Refrigerate for later use.

9.12 Basic recipe for a vegetable soup, nutritious

Reduces blood pressure, strengthens immune system, prevents cancer, forcing spleen, dissolves stagnation, promotes weight loss. Good to fight immunodeficiency, high blood pressure, depressions, diabetes, diarrhea, reduces blood lipids.
Cooking time approx. 2-3 hours
Calories p. portion: 48
5 portions
Allergens: L

Quantity of ingredients
Olive oil 1 table spoon / 4g. (yes)
Onion white 1 piece / 60g. (yes)
Carrot 3 pieces / 200g. (recommended)
Parsnip 3/8 lbs - 6oz / 150g. (yes)
Celery root 1 cup / 100g. (recommended)

Ginger fresh 1/2 teaspoon / 2g. (yes)
Lemon 1/2 piece / 25g. (yes)
Juniper berry 6 pieces / 6g. (recommended)
Thyme dried 1 pinch / 1g. (yes)
Lovage 1 table spoon / 3g. (yes)
Bay leaf 2 leaves / 1g. (yes)
Salt 1 pinch / 1g. (little)
Water 3 cups / 650g. (yes)

Cooking instructions:
Cut the vegetables into cubes.
Heat oil in hot pot, fry shortly onions and vegetables.
Add cold water, then add ginger, bay leaf and lemon juice.
Season with juniper, thyme and lovage. Cover for 2 - 3 hours on a low heat and simmer.
The used vegetables should be thrown away.
The basic recipe serves as a soup base and to refine vegetables, legumes or cereals.
If you want to eat vegetable soup immediately, add the desired vegetables half an hour before.
Refrigerate for later use.

9.13 Basmati rice + Zucchini tofu dish

Diuretic, supports urination, harmonizes spleen and stomach, reduces flatulence, good to fight body overweight and high blood pressure.
Antioxidativ, promotes digestion, perspiration, reduces blood lipids, forcing spleen.
Cooking time approx. 20 min
Calories p. portion: 146
4 portions
Allergens: E

Quantity of ingredients
Soy Tofu 5/8 lbs - 8oz / 250g. (yes)
Olive oil 2 table spoons / 6g. (yes)
Coriander 1/2 teaspoon / 4g. (yes)
Ginger fresh 1/2 teaspoon / 4g. (yes)
Rice Basmati 1/2 cup / 60g. (yes)
Water 3 cups / 200g. (yes)
Zucchini 1 piece / 700g. (recommended)

Cooking instructions:
Cut tofu cubes and marinate with olive oil, tamari, crushed coriander and ginger. Leave at least 1 hour.

Cook Basmati rice with the water. You can season with onion and cardamom.
Roast zucchini and tofu in pan in the hot oil for approx. 5-7 min.
Serve rice and tofu on a plate.
Add the parsley.

Can also be used as a salad for the home and on the go.

9.14 Beef broth

Warming and nourishing, forces.
Cooking time approx. 2-6 hours
Calories p. portion: 125
7 portions
Allergens: L

Quantity of ingredients
Water 4 cup / 1000g. (yes)
Lemon 2 dashes / 2g. (yes)
Beef meat 1,1 lbs / 500g. (yes)
Beef meatbones 2 pieces / 0g. (yes)
Turmeric (yellow root) 1 pinch / 1g. (yes)
Carrot 2 pieces / 100g. (recommended)
Celery root 1 inch / 25g. (recommended)
Parsley root 1 piece / 150g. (yes)
Onion white 1 piece / 50g. (yes)
Bay leaf 2-3 leaves / 2g. (yes)
Coriander 1/2 teaspoon / 2g. (yes)
Ginger fresh 1 inch / 2g. (yes)
Wakame 1 inch / 1g. (yes)
Parsley 1 stem / 10g. (yes)

Cooking instructions:
In a saucepan with water (enough to cover the meat), add a few drops of lemon juice, a little turmeric, beef and bones, heat till it boils and simmer for a while; then pour away the whole broth, clean the pot, rinse off meat and bones with hot water (this will save you from foaming) and put it back to the saucepan with hot water (amount as you like); add a good pinch of turmeric, carrot, celery, parsley root to the pot; add onion,

bay leaves, coriander, a piece of sliced ginger, a strip of wakame, a stalk of parsley; boil everything together and simmer for 2-6 hours (if the meat is to be used otherwise, take it out of the broth after 1 1/2 - 2 hours, as soon as it is cooked, the bones are returned to the broth); When the cooking time is over, pour the broth through a sieve and discard all ingredients.

Notes: The longer the broth has cooked, the warmer but more nourishing it is. It is after cooling for 3-4 days in the refrigerator durable. The broth can be drunk hot or used as a base for soups with cereals, potatoes and fresh vegetables.

9.15 Beef salad

Strengths spleen and stomach, strengthens blood, strengthens the muscles, tendons and bones, diuretic, detoxifying, suppresses conversion of sugar into fat, lowers cholesterol, dissolves stagnation.
Cooking time approx. 10 min
Calories p. portion: 249
1 portions
Allergens: O

Quantity of ingredients
Beef meat 1/8 lbs - 2oz / 50g. (yes)
Onion white 1/2 oz / 20g. (yes)
Peppers 1 oz / 30g. (recommended)
Cucumber (spicy cucumber) 1 oz / 30g. (recommended)
Vinegar (Apple vinegar) 2 teaspoons / 5g. (yes)
Rapeseed oil 2 teaspoons / 5g. (recommended)
Salt 1 pinch / 0,5g. (little)
Pepper (ground) 1 pinch / 0,1g. (yes)
Chives 1 table spoon / 7g. (yes)
Bread with carob kernel flour 2 slices / 50g. (recommended)

Cooking instructions:
Cook the meat with the basic recipe of a beef broth and let it cool down. Cut into 1 cm slices. Cut the onions into rings, pepper and gherkin into small cubes. Mix all ingredients.
Make the salad marinade with vinegar, oil and salt and pour over, season to taste and strain.

9.16 Bitter lemon drink

Appetizing
Cooking time approx. 5 min
Calories p. portion: 130
1 portions
Allergens:

Quantity of ingredients
Bitter Lemon 1 cup / 250g. (yes)

9.17 Blueberry puree

Bilberry is laxative. Clove dissolves stagnation. Cinnamon powder heats stomach and spleen, improves blood circulation.
Cooking time approx. 10 min
Calories p. portion: 10
1 portions
Allergens:

Quantity of ingredients
Blueberry 1/2 oz / 20g. (yes)
Cinnamon ground 1 pinch / 0,1g. (yes)
Clove 1 piece / 1g. (yes)
Water 1 cup / 250g. (yes)

Cooking instructions:
Boil blueberries with cinnamon and clove in water for 10 minutes. Remove the cinnamon and clove. Puree. Sweet as desired.

9.18 Boiled celery salad with exotic spices

Forcing spleen, relieves diarrhea, antibacterial, blood-forming, blood detoxifying, reduces inflammation, diuretic, improves blood circulation.
Cooking time approx. 30 min
Calories p. portion: 166
4 portions
Allergens: GLMNO

Quantity of ingredients
Celery root 1 1/2 piece / 900g. (recommended)
Yogurt (natural, 3.5% fat) 1 cup / 250g. (yes)
Sour cream 15% fat 2 table spoons / 20g. (yes)
Turmeric (yellow root) 1 pinch / 1g. (yes)
Sesame oil 1 table spoon / 20g. (recommended)
Pepper (ground) 1 pinch / 0,5g. (yes)
Lemongrass 1 pinch / 1g. (yes)
Onion white 1/2 piece / 25g. (yes)
Mustard 1/2 teaspoon / 1g. (yes)
Black caraway 1 pinch / 1g. (yes)
Salt 1 pinch / 1g. (little)
Lemon juice 1 piece / 40g. (yes)
Apple (sour) 1/2 piece / 100g. (recommended)
Peppers powder 1 pinch / 1g. (yes)
Vinegar (Apple vinegar) 1 dash / 3g. (yes)

Cooking instructions:
Cook the peeled celeriac in thick slices and then cut into bite-sized strips.

Dressing: Mix a little yoghurt, sour cream, turmeric, sesame oil, pepper, lemongrass powder, finely chopped onion, a little mustard, salt, crushed black cumin, some cold water, lemon juice or vinegar; add the sour chopped apple, some rose paprika, the lukewarm celery and mix well; let it rest for 2 - 3 hours or overnight.
Ideal as a substitute for raw food

9.19 Breakfast - low protein

Increase appetite, detoxifying, increases blood glucose levels, harmonizes heart rhythm, good to fight vomiting, nutritional disorders, diarrhea.
Cooking time approx. 10 min
Calories p. portion: 575
1 portions
Allergens: GO

Quantity of ingredients
Bread with carob kernel flour 3 oz / 80g. (recommended)
Butter organic 1/2 oz / 20g. (yes)
Apricot jam 1 oz / 30g. (yes)
Fresh cheese with herbs 1 oz / 30g. (yes)

Coffee 1/2 cup / 150g. (yes)
Sugar white 1/2 oz / 10g. (little)

Cooking instructions:
Prepare coffee to taste, make fresh cheese if possible with fresh herbs yourself.

9.20 Breakfast - Rice with fruits

Good to fight blood circulation disorders, thrombose, risk of embolism, high blood pressure, a headache, heart attack and stroke. Encourages blood build-up, promotes digestion, reduces Inflammation.
Cooking time approx. 10 min - 3 hours
Calories p. portion: 231
3 portions
Allergens: GHO

Quantity of ingredients
Basic recipe for a rice soup (Congee) 6 cups / 500g. (yes)
Cow's milk (whole milk 3.5% fat) 1/2 to 1 cup / 80g. (yes)
Honey 1 table spoon / 10g. (yes)
Butter organic 1 table spoon / 15g. (yes)
Dates dried 1 table spoon / 15g. (yes)
Fig 1 table spoon / 15g. (yes)
Apple (sour) 1 piece / 200g. (recommended)
Hazelnuts 1/2 teaspoon / 5g. (yes)
Almond 1/2 teaspoon / 5g. (yes)
Cinnamon ground 1 pinch / 1g. (yes)

Cooking instructions:
Cook rice congee according to basic recipe or use pre-cooked.
Make it with the milk more fluid and sweet with honey.
Fry the fruits and nuts in butter and mix with the finished rice soup, add chopped dates, figs and the apple.

9.21 Broccoli cream soup

Strengthen your immune system, build and maintain healthy bones, teeth, hair and nails. Reduces blood pressure, strengthens immune system, prevents cancer, reduces radiation damage.
Cooking time approx. 30 min
Calories p. portion: 98
6 portions
Allergens: LO

Quantity of ingredients
Olive oil 2 table spoons / 7g. (yes)
Broccoli 1,1 lbs / 500g. (recommended)
Carrot 2 pieces / 150g. (recommended)
Potato 2 pieces / 120g. (yes)
Onion white 1 piece / 50g. (yes)
Water 1 cup / 50g. (yes)
Basic recipe for a vegetable soup (nutritious) 2 cup / 500g. (yes)
White wine 1/2 cup / 125g. (little)
Sage 1 teaspoon / 2g. (yes)
Rosemary 1 teaspoon / 2g. (yes)
Pepper (ground) 1 pinch / 0,5g. (yes)
Salt 1 pinch / 1g. (little)

Cooking instructions:
Add the olive oil to the pan, add the washed and cut broccoli, diced carrots and potatoes, sauté for a short time, add the chopped onion, fill with water, enough water to cover the vegetables at least 3 finger breadths. Add bouillon, salt, add a little bit of white wine, add the seasoned sage and rosemary.
Heat till it boils and then simmer on a small fire for about 25 minutes. Season with pepper, if necessary season with sea salt. Purée the soup.

9.22 Carrot soup

Promotes spleen and liver, reduces blood pressure, strengthens immune system, prevents cancer, reduces radiation damage, improves blood circulation, improves medication effect, increase Appetite, stimulates liver function.
Cooking time approx. 30 min
Calories p. portion: 210
2 portions
Allergens: O

Quantity of ingredients
Carrot 1,1 lbs / 500g. (recommended)
Pepper (ground) 1 pinch / 0,5g. (yes)
Nutmeg 1 pinch / 1g. (yes)
Salt 1 pinch / 1g. (little)
White wine 1/2 cup / 125g. (little)
Orange juice Alternatively for wine / g. (yes)
Parsley 2 table spoons / 10g. (yes)

Peppers powder 1 pinch / 1g. (yes)
Thyme dried Alternative to rose paprika / g. (yes)
Pine nuts 1 table spoon / 15g. (yes)
Sunflower seeds Alternatively to pine nuts / g. (yes)

Cooking instructions:
Place peeled large cut carrot pieces in hot water; cook and then puree;
season with ground pepper, a little nutmeg, a pinch of salt; add a dash
of white wine and simmer for a few minutes or season with orange
juice; Add parsley as desired;
stir in some rose paprika or fresh thyme; sprinkle with roasted pine nuts
or sunflower seeds before serving.

9.23 Celery and potato cream soup

Reduces blood pressure, strengthens immune system, promotes weight
loss. Good to fight immunodeficiency, loss of appetite, flatulence,
depressions, diabetes, diarrhea, improves digestion.
Cooking time approx. 45 min
Calories p. portion: 113
4 portions
Allergens: GL

Quantity of ingredients
Olive oil 1 table spoon / 10g. (yes)
Onion white 1/2 piece / 25g. (yes)
Basic recipe for a vegetable soup (nutritious) 3 cups / 700g. (yes)
Potato 5/8 oz / 200g. (yes)
Nutmeg 1 pinch / 0,5g. (yes)
Ground 1 pinch / 0,5g. (yes)
Lemon peel 1/4 piece / 1g. (yes)
Créme fraiche cheese 2 table spoons / 20g. (yes)
Salt 1 pinch / 1g. (little)
Parsley 1 table spoon / 8g. (yes)

Cooking instructions:
Heat the olive oil in a saucepan lightly. Fry the onions very gently in a
mild heat. Pour with vegetable stock according to the basic recipe.
Cover and cook for 15 minutes.
Add curd-cut potato, celery, nutmeg, cumin and lemon zest. Spice with
salt and cook for 12 minutes. Potatoes and celery should be soft.
Remove the lemon peel.
Puree the soup with crème fraiche using a blender. Season the soup

with salt.
Arrange the soup in portions with the chopped parsley.

9.24 Champignon rice

Strengthens kidney, diuretic, warming the body from the inside, expands blood vessels, strengthens the muscles, promotes digestion and is good to fight high blood pressure, dissolves stagnation, promotes weight loss. Good to fight immunodeficiency, loss of appetite.
Cooking time approx. 30 min
Calories p. portion: 410
2 portions
Allergens: L

Quantity of ingredients
Onion white 1 piece / 50g. (yes)
Bay leaf 2 pieces / 1g. (yes)
Clove 2 pieces / 1g. (yes)
Basic recipe for a vegetable soup (nutritious) 7/8 lbs / 350g. (yes)
Rice (whole grain) 5/8 oz / 200g. (yes)
Champignon 1/8 lbs - 2oz / 60g. (yes)
Parsley 1/2 oz / 20g. (yes)
Pepper (ground) 1 pinch / 0,2g. (yes)

Cooking instructions:
Plug in the cloves in the onion. Heat the vegetable stock with the onion and the bay leaves till it boils. Add the rice to the boiling liquid, reduce the temperature to the lowest level and stir with the lid closed for 20-25 minutes.
In the meantime, wash the mushrooms, clean them, slice them, sauté briefly with a little water or sauté. Wash the parsley and chop finely. Remove the onion from the rice, add the mushrooms and the parsley, season with pepper.

9.25 Cola drink

Good to fight lack of appetite, changed sense of taste.
Cooking time approx. 1 min
Calories p. portion: 150
1 portions
Allergens:

Quantity of ingredients
Cola drink 1 cup / 250g. (little)

9.26 Cold cherry soup with curd cheese dumpling

Improves blood circulation, reduces inflammation, good to fight weakness, belching, diabetes, acute or chronic obstruction of the bowel. Laxative, stimulates digestion, cleans the intestinal flora.
Cooking time approx. 2 hours and more
Calories p. portion: 320
2 portions
Allergens: GO

Quantity of ingredients
Cherry compote 7/8 lbs / 450g. (yes)
Agar agar (kelp) 1/2 teaspoon / 1,5g. (yes)
Curd cheese 20% 1/4 lbs - 4oz / 100g. (recommended)
Sour cream 15% fat 1/8 lbs - 2oz / 50g. (yes)
Vanilla sugar natural 1 package / 1g. (yes)
Sugar brown 1 table spoon / 10g. (little)
Cinnamon ground 1 pinch / 0,5g. (yes)
Lemon peel 1 pinch / 1g. (yes)

Cooking instructions:
Strain the cherry compote.
Finely puree half of the cherries with the cherry juice using a blender and pass through a sieve.
Stir agar agar powder with cold water until smooth.
Bring the cherry puree to boil while stirring.
Mix in the agar-agar and cook the cherry puree for 1 minute while stirring.
Spread hot cherry puree on two soup plates.
Sprinkle the remaining cherries into the soup.
Cool down cherry soup for 2 hours until lightly gelled.
Use the hand mixer to stir the cord cheese, sour cream, sugar, vanilla sugar, cinnamon and lemon zest into a smooth, firm cream.
From the cream with the tablespoon, prick small dumplings and put them into the cherry soup.

9.27 Compote from rhubarb

Antipyretic, analgesic, detoxifying, bactericide.
Cooking time approx. 15 min
Calories p. portion: 48
1 portions
Allergens:

Quantity of ingredients
Rhubarb 1/4 lbs - 4oz / 100g. (recommended)
Water 1 cup / 120g. (yes)
Honey 1 table spoon / 10g. (yes)

Cooking instructions:
Wash rhubarb and cut small. Boil in the water. Allow to cool a little and add the honey.

9.28 Compote of local fruit and dried fruit

Promotes digestion, supports urination, stops diarrhea, promotes digestion, appetizing, relieves diarrhea. Warms stomach and spleen, improves blood circulation.
Cooking time approx. 15 min
Calories p. portion: 45
4 portions
Allergens:

Quantity of ingredients
Apple (sweet) 1 piece / 150g. (recommended)
Pear 1 piece / 150g. (recommended)
Cinnamon ground 1 pinch / 0,2g. (yes)
Lemon peel 1/2 teaspoon / 2g. (yes)
Water 2 cup / 500g. (yes)

Cooking instructions:
Cook the apple and pear with the dried fruit until soft. Sprinkle with cinnamon and lemon zest (organic).

9.29 Corn coffee with cardamom

Diuretic, forcing spleen, supports urination, relaxes, reduces fat.
Cooking time approx. 5 min
Calories p. portion: 3
1 portions
Allergens:

Quantity of ingredients
Cereal coffee 1 table spoon / 15g. (yes)
Cardamom 2 cores / 1g. (yes)
Water 1 cup / 120g. (yes)

Cooking instructions:
Boil water, coffee, sugar and cardamom. Let it set for one min before drinking.

9.30 Cottage cheese with steamed fruit

Good to fight loss of appetite, promotes digestion, supports urination.
Cooking time approx. 20 min
Calories p. portion: 214
2 portions
Allergens: G

Quantity of ingredients
Cottage cheese 3/4 lbs / 300g. (yes)
Apple (sour) 1 piece / 100g. (recommended)
Pear 1 piece / 100g. (recommended)

Cooking instructions:
Wash apples and pears well, do not peel, and chop small. In a pot with steam filter, boil them al dente, remove and allow to cool down.
Serve the cheese, spread the fruit on it.

9.31 Cranberry yogurt mix

Good to fight acute or chronic constipation of the intestine, oral mucosal inflammation, diarrhea, flatulence, throat irritation.
Cooking time approx. 5 min
Calories p. portion: 57
2 portions
Allergens: GO

Quantity of ingredients
Yogurt (natural, 1.5% fat) 1/4 lbs - 4oz / 125g. (recommended)
Cranberry jam 2 table spoons / 20g. (yes)
Mineral water 1 cup / 250g. (yes)

Cooking instructions:
Mix yoghurt, cranberry jam and mineral water until frothy.

9.32 Cucumber salad

Diuretic, detoxifying, suppresses conversion of sugar into fat, lowers
cholesterol, prevents cancer. Cucumber cools and moistens. Dill works
against flatulence, anticonvulsant in gastrointestinal discomfort.
Cooking time approx. 5 min
Calories p. portion: 27
2 portions
Allergens: O

Quantity of ingredients
Cucumber 1 piece / 400g. (recommended)
Salt 1 pinch / 1g. (little)
Dill 1 pinch / 1g. (yes)
Vinegar (Apple vinegar) 1 table spoon / 10g. (yes)

Cooking instructions:
Cut the cucumber (do not peel the BIO) thinly and season.

9.33 Cucumber soup

Diuretic, detoxifying, suppresses conversion of sugar into fat, lowers
cholesterol, prevents cancer, promotes digestion, diaphoretic, dries out,
good to fight yeast infections.
Cooking time approx. 20 min
Calories p. portion: 96
4 portions
Allergens: M

Quantity of ingredients
Olive oil 2 table spoons / 35g. (yes)
Cucumber 2 pieces / 400g. (recommended)
Water 2 cup / 500g. (yes)
Sage 3 leaves / 3g. (yes)
Mustard 1/2 teaspoon / 0,5g. (yes)
Coriander 1 pinch / 1g. (yes)
Cardamom 1 pinch / 1g. (yes)
Salt 1 pinch / 1g. (little)

Cooking instructions:
Heat oil and roast short the small cucumbers. Add Mustard seeds, coriander, cardamom and salt. Add water. Simmer for 10-15 min. Puree and decorate with fresh chopped sage.

9.34 Curry rice with raisins and nuts

Stops diarrhea, promotes digestion, appetizing, harmonizes the stomach, improves blood circulation, improves medication effect, stimulates appetite, detoxifies the skin, stimulates nerves, frees breathing, increases body temperature, promotes perspiration.
Cooking time approx. 30 min
Calories p. portion: 275
4 portions
Allergens: HO

Quantity of ingredients
Sunflower oil 1 table spoon / 15g. (yes)
Onion white 1 piece / 50g. (yes)
Curry 1/2 teaspoon / 2g. (yes)
Rice wild (nature rice) 1 cup / 120g. (yes)
Salt 1 pinch / 1g. (little)
White wine 1/2 cup / 125g. (little)
Lemon Alternatively for white wine / g. (yes)
Peppers powder 1 pinch / 1g. (yes)
Apple (sweet) 2 pieces / 300g. (recommended)
Raisins 2 table spoons / 25g. (yes)
Walnuts 2 table spoons / 25g. (recommended)
Water 6 cups / 500g. (yes)

Cooking instructions:
Heat oil in a pot; fry chopped onions until glassy; add the curry and let it foam for a short time; then fry the raw rice for a few minutes over a

gentle heat, stirring constantly; Salt, a dash of white wine or lemon juice, rose paprika, sweet apples chopped, raisins, chopped, roasted nuts added; pour hot water on it until well covered; simmer until the rice is cooked.

Goes well with: carrot and fennel vegetables, legumes with boiled vegetables, sliced poultry with ginger and mushrooms.

9.35 Delicately spiced zucchini with tomatoes

Diuretic, promotes digestion, helps to digest fat, reduces blood pressure, dissolves stagnation, antioxidativ, supports urination, diuretic, warming the body from the inside, expands blood vessels.
Cooking time approx. 10 min
Calories p. portion: 203
4 portions
Allergens:

Quantity of ingredients
Olive oil 1 table spoon / 20g. (yes)
Onion white 2 pieces / 120g. (yes)
Zucchini 4 pieces / 800g. (recommended)
Oregano dried 1 pinch / 1g. (yes)
Basil (fresh) 6-8 leaves / 3g. (yes)
Salt 1 pinch / 1g. (little)
Tomato 2 pieces / 120g. (recommended)
Rice (whole grain) 1 cup / 120g. (yes)
Water 6 cups / 400g. (yes)
Salt 1 pinch / 1g. (little)

Cooking instructions:
In a hot pan, fry olive oil, finely chopped onions and finely chopped zucchini until half cooked. Add plenty of dried oregano. Salt and chop the tomatoes for a few minutes until the zucchini are tender but crisp. Add fresh basil as desired.

Variation: Put some sheep's cheese over the tomatoes and finish cooking with the lid closed.

Place the rice in salted water, heat till it boils and let it simmer over low heat for about 15 minutes.

9.36 Duck with mung beans

Strengthens blood, forcing spleen, supports urination, promotes spleen and liver, reduces blood pressure, strengthens immune system, prevents cancer, reduces radiation damage, dissolves stagnation.
Cooking time approx. 2 hours
Calories p. portion: 747
5 portions
Allergens: E

Quantity of ingredients
Duck (slaughtered) 1/2 piece / 1250g. (yes)
Onion white 2 pieces / 120g. (yes)
Carrot 1 piece / 120g. (recommended)
Garlic 1 clove / 3g. (yes)
Mung bean 5/8 lbs - 8oz / 250g. (yes)
Peppercorns 3 pieces / 2g. (yes)
Honey 1 teaspoon / 3g. (yes)
Soy sauce 1 teaspoon / 3g. (yes)
Lemon juice 1 teaspoon / 3g. (yes)
Salt 1 pinch / 1g. (little)
Pepper (ground) 1 pinch / 0,5g. (yes)
Olive oil 1 table spoon / 10g. (yes)
Bay leaf 2 leaves / 2g. (yes)
Black caraway 1 pinch / 1g. (yes)
Savory 1 teaspoon / 2g. (recommended)

Cooking instructions:
The day before soak the mung beans and rinse the duck cold. Wash the vegetables, clean and cut into pieces. Put the duck and vegetables in a saucepan and cover with water. Add bay leaves, savory, mugwort and peppercorns. Boil over medium heat and simmer for 45 minutes. Skim off the foam. Remove duck from the stock, allow to cool and keep cool overnight.

In a saucepan, sauté the chopped onion in olive oil and pour in 1/4 liter of stock and add the pre-cooked vegetables. Add the mung beans and season with honey, soy sauce, lemon juice, salt, crushed black cumin and pepper.

Serve with rice or potatoes.

9.37 Fennel-Rice Soup

Forcing spleen, relieves constipation, stimulates nerves, detoxifying, reduces inflammation, improves blood circulation.
Cooking time approx. 15-20 min
Calories p. portion: 156
2 portions
Allergens: EG

Quantity of ingredients
Basic recipe for a rice soup (Congee) 1 cup / 300g. (yes)
Fennel 1/2 piece / 150g. (recommended)
Butter organic 1 table spoon / 15g. (yes)
Soy sauce 1 dash / 3g. (yes)

Cooking instructions:
Cook the fennel softly in the rice soup according to the basic recipe.
Before serving, add a piece of butter and some soy sauce.

9.38 Figs with mozzarella and honey

Promotes digestion, reduces inflammation, bloating and nausea, relaxing and reassuring, relieves pain, detoxifying, blood stilling, forcing spleen and digestive system, detoxifying, bactericide.
Cooking time approx. 10 min
Calories p. portion: 415
1 portions
Allergens: GO

Quantity of ingredients
Fig 4 pieces / 100g. (yes)
Mozzarella 1 piece / 50g. (yes)
Basil (fresh) 1/2 bunch / 50g. (yes)
Honey 2 table spoons / 24g. (yes)
Pepper (ground) 1 pinch / 0,1g. (yes)
Grapeseed oil 1 table spoon / 12g. (yes)
Vinegar Aceto Balsamico white 1 table spoon / 12g. (yes)

Cooking instructions:
Quarter fresh figs, dice buffalo mozzarella, pluck basil leaves.
Mix a dressing with light balsamic vinegar, grapeseed oil and honey and season to taste.

Place the figs on the edge of the appropriate plate. Spread the mozzarella cubes and season with black pepper.
Spread whole or roughly sliced basil leaves over it and moisten with the marinade.
Spiced pizza bread goes perfectly with it.

9.39 Fish soup with rosemary

Promotes spleen and liver, reduces blood pressure, strengthens immune system, prevents cancer, reduces radiation damage, has little cholesterol and is protein rich, improves blood circulation, increases appetite. Antioxidant, forcing spleen, dissolves stagnation.
Cooking time approx. 30 min
Calories p. portion: 271
4 portions
Allergens: DLO

Quantity of ingredients
Basic recipe for a fish soup 2 cup / 500g. (yes)
Rosemary 1/2 bunch / 7g. (yes)
Onion (spring onion) 1 piece / 20g. (yes)
Olive oil 2 table spoons / 35g. (yes)
Fish pieces mixed (fresh water) 5/8 lbs - 8oz / 250g. (recommended)
Carrot 1 piece / 120g. (recommended)
Parsnip 1 piece / 180g. (yes)
Celery root 1 slice / 20g. (recommended)
Salt 1 pinch / 1g. (little)
Peppercorns 2 pieces / 1g. (yes)
Garlic 1 clove / 3g. (yes)

Cooking instructions:
Fry the onion and garlic in oil. Add fish broth. Add diced carrots, parsnips and celery. Season with salt and peppercorns. Simmer the soup on a low heat for 25 minutes.
Wash the fish, drizzle with lemon juice, divide into pieces and add to the soup with the pink rosemary. Cook for 5 min on low heat.
Add the chives and parsley and season the soup with the salt.

9.40 Fried apple

Good to fight acute or chronic constipation of the intestine, warming stomach and spleen, improves blood circulation. Good to fight kidney weakness, back pain and abdominal pain, impotence.
Cooking time approx. 30 min
Calories p. portion: 408
4 portions
Allergens: GH

Quantity of ingredients
Apple (sour) 4 pieces / 500g. (recommended)
Hazelnuts 1/8 lbs - 2oz / 50g. (yes)
Almond 1/8 lbs - 2oz / 50g. (yes)
Cinnamon ground 1 pinch / 0,2g. (yes)
Vanilla sugar natural 1 package / 3g. (yes)
Cow's milk (whole milk 3.5% fat) 2 table spoons / 24g. (yes)
Sugar - icing sugar 2 table spoons / 36g. (little)
Cinnamon ground 1 pinch / 1g. (yes)
Yoghurt vanilla 3 cups / 750g. (yes)

Cooking instructions:
Wash the apples, cut off a lid, cut out the core casing with a teaspoon so that the apple remains a tight bottom.
Mix nuts, almonds, fructose, milk, vanilla sugar, cinnamon well. Fill into the apples. Put the covers back on.
Bake in preheated oven at 180 ° C for approx. 20 minutes.
Mix icing sugar and cinnamon.
Spread vanilla yoghurt on plate, place 1 baked apple on each, sprinkle with cinnamon-powdered sugar mixture.
Serve hot immediately!

9.41 Grated apple

Eat 3 times a day - Apple (sour) scraped and brown is stuffing. Relieves diarrhea.
Cooking time approx. 10 min
Calories p. portion: 120
1 portions
Allergens:

Quantity of ingredients
Apple (sour) 1 piece / 200g. (recommended)

Cooking instructions:
Peel apple and grate as fine as possible. Leave for at least 5 minutes until it turns brown.

9.42 Halibut with tomato and garlic sauce

Promotes digestion, helps to digest fat, supports urination, reduces blood pressure, good to fight rheumatism, flatulence, bladder weakness, anemia, high blood pressure, depressions, diabetes, diarrhea. Valuable omega-3 fatty acids.
Cooking time approx. 45 min
Calories p. portion: 319
5 portions
Allergens: D

Quantity of ingredients
Rice variety any 1 cup / 120g. (yes)
Water 6 cups / 240g. (yes)
Salt 1 pinch / 1g. (little)
Halibut (Flatfish) 2,2 lbs / 800g. (yes)
Salt 1 pinch / 1g. (little)
Pepper (ground) 1 pinch / 0,5g. (yes)
Lemon juice 1 dash / 2g. (yes)
Bay leaf 2 pieces / 2g. (yes)
Lemon 1 piece / 30g. (yes)
Garlic 8 pieces / 10g. (yes)
Thyme dried 1 table spoon / 5g. (yes)
Olives 0,2 lbs / 75g. (yes)
Tomato 4 pieces / 200g. (recommended)
Salt 1 pinch / 1g. (little)
Pepper (ground) 1 pinch / 0,5g. (yes)

Cooking instructions:
Cook rice with salted water (1:3).
Rinse the fish under running cold water, dab with kitchen paper and rub with salt, pepper and lemon juice.
Place the fish fillets in a casserole dish with pieces of bay leaf.
Wash the lemon hot and cut into slices, peel and halve the garlic.
Sprinkle the olives and the thyme over them.
Brew the tomatoes with hot water, skin and chop.
Mix all ingredients, season with salt and pepper and distribute around

the fish.
Cook everything at 200°C/392°F for about 20 minutes.
Serve with the rice.

9.43 Hungarian rice salad

Promotes digestion, helps to digest fat, supports urination, reduces blood pressure, strengthens kidney and bladder, diuretic, warming the body from the inside, expands blood vessels, strengthens the muscles, regulates internal organs functions.
Cooking time approx. 25 min
Calories p. portion: 421
2 portions
Allergens: GM

Quantity of ingredients
Rice (whole grain) 1/2 cup / 60g. (yes)
Water 3 cups / 300g. (yes)
Salt 1 pinch / 0,3g. (little)
Tomato 1/4 lbs - 4oz / 100g. (recommended)
Peppers 1/8 lbs - 2oz / 50g. (recommended)
Champignon 1 oz / 30g. (yes)
Edam cheese 1 oz / 30g. (yes)
Yogurt (natural, 1.5% fat) 1/8 lbs - 2oz / 45g. (recommended)
Salt 1 pinch / 1g. (little)
Herbs various 1 table spoon / 8g. (yes)
Rapeseed oil 2 table spoons / 20g. (recommended)
Mustard 1 teaspoon / 3g. (yes)
Pepper (ground) 1 pinch / 0,2g. (yes)

Cooking instructions:
Pour the rice into plenty of boiling salt water and let it drain gently. Wash tomatoes and peppers and core. Cut both in to small cubes. Peel the mushrooms (from the tin or with rapeseed oil for a short time) and cut the cheese into small cubes and add to the rice. Prepare the marinade and mix with the ingredients, refrigerate and leave for at least an hour.

9.44 Kohlrabi in chervil sauce with potatoes

Reduces inflammation, lowers cholesterol, diuretic, conducts bowel winds, strengthens immune system, prevents cancer, promotes weight

loss. Good to fight loss of appetite, flatulence, high blood pressure, depressions, diabetes, diarrhea.
Cooking time approx. 1 hour
Calories p. portion: 188
4 portions
Allergens: GL

Quantity of ingredients
Potato 6 pieces / 450g. (yes)
Basic recipe for a vegetable soup (nutritious) 1 cup / 300g. (yes)
Potato 1/4 lbs - 4oz / 100g. (yes)
Nutmeg 1 pinch / 0,2g. (yes)
Lemon peel 1/2 teaspoon / 2g. (yes)
Ginger fresh 1/2 teaspoon / 2g. (yes)
Lovage 1/2 teaspoon / 2g. (yes)
Kohlrabi 3/4 lbs / 300g. (recommended)
Salt 1 pinch / 1g. (little)
Pepper (ground) 1 pinch / 0,2g. (yes)
Sour cream 15% fat 2 table spoons / 30g. (yes)
Chervil dried 1 Bunch / 80g. (yes)

Cooking instructions:
Boil the potatoes in salted water.
Bring half of the vegetable stock to boil. Add the diced potatoes, nutmeg, lemon zest, ginger and lovage. Cover the potatoes and cook for about 10 minutes until soft and puree them with a blender until they are smooth.
Bring remaining vegetable stock to boil. Cut kohlrabi into cubes and add, cover and cook for about 8 minutes. Stir in the potato sauce and heat everything briefly.
Puree with the mixing stick chervil and sour cream. Mix the chervil cream with the kohlrabi vegetables.
Serve with the cooked, peeled potatoes.

9.45 Leek and potato gratin

Reduces inflammation, improves digestion, regenerates skin, supports urination, lowers cholesterol, promotes sweating, dissolves stagnation.
Cooking time approx. 1 hour
Calories p. portion: 368
4 portions
Allergens: CGL

Quantity of ingredients
Potato 1,1 lbs / 500g. (yes)
Leek 1,1 lbs / 500g. (yes)
Apple (sour) 1 piece / 200g. (recommended)
Créme fraiche cheese 1/4 lbs - 4oz / 125g. (yes)
Basic recipe for a vegetable soup (nutritious) 1/4 cup / 20g. (yes)
Chicken yolk 1 piece / 20g. (little)
Emmental cheese 2 table spoons / 20g. (yes)
Salt 1 pinch / 1g. (little)
Pepper (ground) 1 pinch / 0,5g. (yes)

Cooking instructions:
Wash the potatoes, peel, cut into very thin slices and pat dry. Place half in a flat greased baking dish.
Clean and wash leeks and cut into fine rings. Wash apple, peel and cut into thin slices. Spread the leek rings and apple slices on top. Put the remaining potato slices on top.
Mix crème fraiche, egg yolk, grated Emmentaler, salt and pepper, if necessary add some vegetable stock and pour over the casserole.
Bake at 200°C/392°F in the oven for about 45 to 50 minutes until golden brown. Cover with parchment paper after 30 minutes to prevent the burr from drying out.

9.46 Lentil and chestnut soup with curry

Reduces blood pressure, strengthens immune system, prevents cancer, reduces radiation damage, forcing spleen, dissolves stagnation, promotes weight loss. Good to fight immunodeficiency, loss of appetite, flatulence, high blood pressure, depressions, diabetes, diarrhea.
Cooking time approx. 45 min
Calories p. portion: 176
4 portions
Allergens: LO

Quantity of ingredients
Lentils red 3/8 lbs - 6oz / 150g. (yes)
Chestnuts 3/8 lbs - 6oz / 150g. (yes)
Olive oil 1 table spoon / 10g. (yes)
Curry 2 teaspoons / 8g. (yes)
Basic recipe for a vegetable soup (nutritious) 2 cup / 500g. (yes)
Turmeric (yellow root) 1 teaspoon / 2g. (yes)
White wine 1/2 cup / 125g. (little)

Salt (herbal) 1 pinch / 1g. (yes)
Anise (Common Fennel) 1 pinch / 1g. (yes)
Cardamom 1 pinch / 1g. (yes)
Cardamom 1 pinch / 0,5g. (yes)
Parsley 2 table spoons / 6g. (yes)

Cooking instructions:
Add the olive oil to a pan, sauté the chestnuts, sprinkle with the curry,
add the lentils and season with vegetable stock, add a little white wine,
mix in the curcuma, simmer for about 20 minutes (until the chestnuts
are tender).
Then puree the soup.
Taste with a pinch of anise, cardamom and herbal salt. At the end,
sprinkle finely chopped parsley over it.

9.47 Lettuce with vinegar dressing

Relieves fatigue, regulates gastrointestinal function, dissolves
stagnation, laxative, antiparasitic, improves blood circulation,
detoxifying, reduces inflammation, relieves pain.
Cooking time approx. 10 min
Calories p. portion: 68
2 portions
Allergens: O

Quantity of ingredients
Lettuce 1 piece / 200g. (recommended)
Vinegar (Apple vinegar) 1 table spoon / 10g. (yes)
Water 1 table spoon / 10g. (yes)
Rapeseed oil 1 table spoon / 10g. (recommended)
Onion (spring onion) 1 piece / 20g. (yes)
Salt 1 pinch / 0,5g. (little)
Pepper (ground) 1 pinch / 0,1g. (yes)
Chives 1 table spoon / 5g. (yes)

Cooking instructions:
Clean lettuce, wash and drain. Add the ingredients to the marinade in
an extra container. Salad with marinade just before consumption. Just
before, sprinkle with chives.

9.48 Mango banana yoghurt drink ice cold

Good to fight loss of appetite, oral mucosa inflammation. Regulates gastrointestinal function, chronic constipation. Prevents cancer. Diuretic, forcing spleen.
Cooking time approx. 5 min
Calories p. portion: 121
2 portions
Allergens: G

Quantity of ingredients
Mango juice 1/2 cup / 100g. (yes)
Yogurt (natural, 1.5% fat) 1/4 lbs - 4oz / 100g. (recommended)
Mineral water 1/2 cup / 100g. (yes)
Banana 1/2 piece / 150g. (yes)
Acerola fruit nectar or powder 1 teaspoon / 2g. (yes)

Cooking instructions:
Mix all the ingredients and 2-3 ice cubes in a blender.

9.49 Marinated cod on pumpkin puree

Reduces inflammation, improves digestion, promotes spleen, lung, stomach and kidneys, diuretic, reduces blood glucose, good to fight constipation and flatulence, dissolves stagnation.
Cooking time approx. 2 hours
Calories p. portion: 202
4 portions
Allergens: DG

Quantity of ingredients
Potato 6 pieces / 400g. (yes)
Pumpkin 5/8 oz / 200g. (yes)
Onion white 1 piece / 50g. (yes)
Oregano dried 1/2 teaspoon / 1g. (yes)
Lemon juice 1/2 piece / 15g. (yes)
Salt 1 pinch / 1g. (little)
Pepper (ground) 1 pinch / 0,3g. (yes)
Créme fraiche cheese 2 table spoons / 30g. (yes)
Yogurt (natural, 1.5% fat) 3/8 lbs - 6oz / 150g. (recommended)
Oregano dried 1/4 teaspoon / 1g. (yes)
Basil (fresh) 1/2 teaspoon / 2g. (yes)

Cod 3/4 lbs / 300g. (recommended)
Salt 1 pinch / 1g. (little)
Pepper (ground) 1 pinch / 0,3g. (yes)
Olive oil 1 teaspoon / 3g. (yes)

Cooking instructions:
Mix yoghurt with oregano, basil and thyme.
Wash the fish fillets, pat dry, place in a flat shape and pour over the marinade. Leave 2 hours in refrigerator.

Cook the potatoes in salted water until soft and peel.
Sauté the onion in oil until glassy, add the diced pumpkin and cook for about 10 min. Add oregano, lemon juice, salt, pepper and crème fraiche and puree with the blender.
Remove fish fillets from the marinade, drain, pat dry and salt. Coat a coated grill pan with 2 teaspoons of oil. Roast the fish fillets on both sides for 3 - 4 minutes and arrange with the potatoes on the pumpkin puree.

9.50 Miso soup with tofu

Vitamins, minerals and secondary plant active ingredients, invigorating, detoxifying, strengthens immune system, promotes digestion, forcing spleen, containing enzymes, reduces flatulence, alginic acid detoxifies the bowel, dissolves stagnation.
Cooking time approx. 5 min
Calories p. portion: 51
3 portions
Allergens: E

Quantity of ingredients
Wakame 1 piece / 5g. (yes)
Miso 3-4 table spoons / 30g. (yes)
Soy Tofu 1/8 lbs - 2oz / 50g. (yes)
Water 2 cup / 500g. (yes)
Soy sauce 1 dash / 3g. (yes)
Onion (spring onion) 1/2 teaspoon / 6g. (yes)

Cooking instructions:
Boil soybean seedlings, wakame algae and diced tofu for 5 minutes.
Put the miso paste in the soup plate and slowly pour over the soup.
Season with Tamari sauce. Sprinkle with cutted spring onion.

9.51 Oven potatoes with celery-curd cheese (quark)

Promotes spleen, reduces Inflammation, improves digestion, regenerates skin, supports urination, lowers cholesterol.
Cooking time approx. 30 min
Calories p. portion: 304
2 portions
Allergens: GL

Quantity of ingredients
Celery root 3 oz / 80g. (recommended)
Basic recipe for a vegetable soup (nutritious) 1/2 cup / 100g. (yes)
Ground caraway 1 pinch / 0,2g. (yes)
Lemon peel 1/2 teaspoon / 1g. (yes)
Salt 1 pinch / 1g. (little)
Pepper (ground) 1 pinch / 0,2g. (yes)
Lemon juice 1 teaspoon / 3g. (yes)
Curd cheese 20% 5/8 oz / 200g. (recommended)
Créme fraiche cheese 1/2 teaspoon / 5g. (yes)
Potato 6 pieces / 400g. (yes)
Olive oil 2 teaspoons / 5g. (yes)
Salt 1 pinch / 1g. (little)

Cooking instructions:
Celery-curd cheese:
Mix celery with vegetable broth according to basic recipe, caraway and lemon peel. Cook for about 8 minutes until the celery is soft and the vegetable broth almost evaporated. Mix the celery vegetable broth with the lemon juice, finely, and stir until smooth. Season with salt and pepper.

Baked potatoes:
Preheat oven to 200 °C / 400 °F.
Brush the potatoes well, halve them, and place them on a baking tray with the cut surface facing up. Lightly salt the surfaces and sprinkle with oil. Fry the potatoes in the oven for about 25 minutes.
Serve the celery plug to the potatoes.

9.52 Paprika-tomato rice

Good to fight little cholesterol, diabetes. Low in protein, low fat content, little protein. Forcing spleen, dissolves stagnation, promotes weight loss. Good to fight immunodeficiency, loss of appetite, flatulence, high blood pressure, depressions.
Cooking time approx. 25 min
Calories p. portion: 291
3 portions
Allergens: L

Quantity of ingredients
Onion white 1 piece / 50g. (yes)
Peppers 4 pieces / 120g. (recommended)
Bay leaf 2 pieces / 1g. (yes)
Clove 2 pieces / 1g. (yes)
Basic recipe for a vegetable soup (nutritious) 7/8 lbs / 400g. (yes)
Rice (whole grain) 5/8 oz / 200g. (yes)
Champignon 1/8 lbs - 2oz / 60g. (yes)
Parsley 1/2 oz / 20g. (yes)
Pepper (ground) 1 pinch / 0,2g. (yes)
Peppers (rose peppers) 1 pinch / 0,2g. (yes)
Tomato 1/4 lbs - 4oz / 120g. (recommended)

Cooking instructions:
Finely chop the onion. Cut the peppers into fine strips.
Heat margarine in a saucepan, sauté onions and peppers, and rice. Add the vegetable stock, add cloves and bay leaves and leave to simmer in a closed pot for approx. 20 minutes. Cut the tomato meat into 1 cm cubes and add to the rice 5 minutes before the end of cooking.

9.53 Pear juice

Promotes digestion, supports urination.
Cooking time approx. 5 min
Calories p. portion: 180
2 portions
Allergens:

Quantity of ingredients
Pear 3 pieces / 600g. (recommended)

Cooking instructions:
Peel pears thinly (vitamins under the skin) and core. Juice in the juicer.

9.54 Potato cream with herbs and fresh cheese

Good to fight loss of appetite, constipation, bloating and nausea.
Improves digestion, supports urination, prevents cancer, forcing spleen,
dissolves stagnation, relaxing and reassuring.
Cooking time approx. 25 min
Calories p. portion: 217
2 portions
Allergens: G

Quantity of ingredients
Potato (mealy) 5/8 lbs - 8oz / 250g. (yes)
Fresh cheese 3 oz / 80g. (yes)
Yogurt (natural, 1.5% fat) 2 table spoons / 45g. (recommended)
Chives 1/2 bunch / 50g. (yes)
Basil (fresh) 1 teaspoon / 4g. (yes)
Parsley 1 teaspoon / 4g. (yes)
Dill 1/2 teaspoon / 2g. (yes)
Salt 1 pinch / 1g. (little)
Black caraway 1 pinch / 0,5g. (yes)
Pepper (ground) 1 pinch / 0,5g. (yes)

Cooking instructions:
Softly steam the potatoes in the pan, peel them and press through the
potato press.
Mix cream cheese, yoghurt and herbs under the potatoes, season with
salt, crushed black cumin and pepper.

9.55 Potato-basil soup

Reduces inflammation, improves digestion, supports urination, lowers
cholesterol, reduces blood pressure, strengthens immune system,
prevents cancer, reduces radiation damage, antioxidativ, dissolves
stagnation.
Cooking time approx. 25 min
Calories p. portion: 96
4 portions
Allergens: L

Quantity of ingredients
Water 2 cups / 450g. (yes)
Potato 4 pieces / 200g. (yes)
Carrot 2 pieces / 100g. (recommended)
Celery root 1 piece / 500g. (recommended)

Pepper (ground) 1 pinch / 0,5g. (yes)
Ground 1 pinch / 1g. (yes)
Garlic 1 clove / 3g. (yes)
Salt 1 pinch / 1g. (little)
Lemon 1 teaspoon / 3g. (yes)
Basil (fresh) 1 Bunch / 50g. (yes)
Peppers powder 1 pinch / 1g. (yes)
Sugar cane sugar 1 pinch / 1g. (little)
Olive oil 1 table spoon / 10g. (yes)

Cooking instructions:
Peeled and chopped 4 medium potatoes in a pot of hot water and 2
chopped medium carrots, a piece of celery root, a pinch of pepper, a
pinch of ground cumin, crushed a small clove of garlic, a pinch of salt, 1
teaspoon of lemon juice, simmer until the Vegetables is soft.

Add 1 bunch finely chopped basil into one half of the soup and puree
everything; stir in the other half of the basil; with rose paprika, a pinch of
whole cane sugar, 1 tablespoon of olive oil or butter, freshly ground
pepper, salt to taste.

9.56 Potatoes with curd cheese sauce

Improves digestion, supports urination, lowers cholesterol. Good to fight
weakness, belching, diabetes, acute or chronic obstruction of the bowel,
skin problems. Good to fight Bloating, cramping in gastrointestinal
complaints.
Cooking time approx. 45 min
Calories p. portion: 414
6 portions
Allergens: G

Quantity of ingredients
Potato 2,2 lbs / 1000g. (yes)
Curd cheese 20% 1,1 lbs / 500g. (recommended)
Cream, sweet 30% 5/8 oz / 200g. (little)
Edam cheese 3 oz / 80g. (yes)
Dill 1 Bunch / 100g. (yes)
Corn germ oil 1 teaspoon / 3g. (recommended)
Pepper (ground) 1 pinch / 0,2g. (yes)
Salt 1/2 teaspoon / 1g. (little)
Sunflower seeds 1/8 lbs - 2oz / 40g. (yes)

Cooking instructions:
Wash the potatoes and cook in plenty of water for about 20 minutes. Stir the creamy cheese with the cream and cottage cheese. Wash the sprouts, finely chop. Stir in with the chopped dill. (For the baby, mix 150 g. of pot with the oil.) Mix the rest with pepper, salt and the sunflower seeds. Peel the potatoes, arrange (for the baby 200 g.) with the pot.

9.57 Pumpkin curry

Promotes digestion and sweating, Dissolves stagnation, strengthens lungs and spleen, diuretic, reduces blood glucose, forcing spleen and digestive system, detoxifying, strengthens the muscles and bones.
Cooking time approx. 20 min
Calories p. portion: 193
3 portions
Allergens:

Quantity of ingredients
Pumpkin 3/4 lbs / 300g. (yes)
Olive oil 2 table spoons / 30g. (yes)
Coriander 1 pinch / 1g. (yes)
Pepper (ground) 1 pinch / 0,5g. (yes)
Curry 1 pinch / 1g. (yes)
Water 1/4 cup / 50g. (yes)
Salt 1 pinch / 1g. (little)
Parsley 1 table spoon / 7g. (yes)
Cardamom 1 pinch / 1g. (yes)
Turmeric (yellow root) 1 pinch / 1g. (yes)
Rice (whole grain) 1/2 cup / 60g. (yes)
Water 3 cups / 300g. (yes)
Salt 1 pinch / 1g. (little)

Cooking instructions:
Heat olive oil in pan. Steam the pumpkin cut in cubes, season with cilantro, pepper and curry, simmer with a little water, salt with sea salt, add chopped parsley with cardamom and turmeric, simmer on a small fire for about 10 minutes, depending on the pumpkin, the pumpkin should still be firm.

Place the rice in salted water, bring to the boil and let it simmer over low heat for about 15 minutes.

9.58 Quick zucchini soup

Diuretic, supports urination. Strengthens gastrointestinal function, expands blood vessels, prevents cancer, prevents diseases (in the elderly). Stimulates liver function, detoxifying.
Cooking time approx. 10 min
Calories p. portion: 42
4 portions
Allergens:

Quantity of ingredients
Zucchini 2-3 pieces / 500g. (recommended)
Onion white 1 piece / 50g. (yes)
Corn germ oil 2 table spoons / 6g. (recommended)
Parsley 1 table spoon / 7g. (yes)
Chives 1 teaspoon / 3g. (yes)
Water 2 cup / 400g. (yes)

Cooking instructions:
Fry chopped onion in oil. Add sliced zucchini and sauté well. Pour with water. Chop parsley and chives, add and puree everything.

9.59 Raw celery salad

Refreshing, forcing spleen, provides Vitamin C, strengthens digestive system, detoxifying, improves blood circulation, strengthens liver and kidney, detoxifying, strengthens the muscles, promotes weight loss.
Cooking time approx. 15 min
Calories p. portion: 590
1 portions
Allergens: HLN

Quantity of ingredients
Celery root 1/4 piece / 125g. (recommended)
Celery sticks 2 branches / 30g. (recommended)
Sesame oil 4 table spoons / 40g. (recommended)
Almond puree 2 table spoons / 20g. (yes)
Pepper (ground) 1 pinch / 0,5g. (yes)
Salt 1 pinch / 1g. (little)
Lemon 1/2 cup / 50g. (yes)
Orange juice 1/2 cup / 60g. (yes)
Peppers powder 1 pinch / 1g. (yes)

Cooking instructions:
Finely grate the celeriac; cut the celeriac into small pieces; celery leaves, cut into small pieces, blanch and combine everything.

Dressing: sesame oil, almond paste, pepper, salt, lemon and fresh orange juice, stir well some rose paprika; mix with the celery and let it pass through.

9.60 Refreshing cucumber soup with potatoes

Diuretic, detoxifying, suppresses conversion of sugar into fat, lowers cholesterol, prevents cancer, reduces inflammation, improves digestion, lowers cholesterol, dissolves stagnation, improves blood circulation, stimulates appetite.
Cooking time approx. 15 min
Calories p. portion: 148
3 portions
Allergens: GN

Quantity of ingredients
Sesame oil 1 table spoon / 10g. (recommended)
Potato 4 pieces / 300g. (yes)
Onion (spring onion) 3 pieces / 60g. (yes)
Pepper (ground) 1 pinch / 0,5g. (yes)
Nutmeg 1 pinch / 1g. (yes)
Salt 1 pinch / 1g. (little)
Lemon 1/2 piece / 25g. (yes)
Cucumber 2 pieces / 500g. (recommended)
Cream, sweet 30% 1 table spoon / 10g. (little)
Dill 1 table spoon / 15g. (yes)

Cooking instructions:
Sauté sesame oil, chopped potatoes, plenty of spring onions in a hot pot; add pepper, a little nutmeg, salt, lemon juice, hot water, diced cucumber; simmer for about 10 minutes and then puree; add some sweet cream as you like, fresh dill.

Variation: Add a little chili, oregano, thyme or rosemary to soften the cooling effect.

9.61 Rhubarb and apple jelly

Antioxidants, lots of vitamin C, laxative, relieves pain, detoxifying, warms stomach and spleen, improves blood circulation.
Cooking time approx. 15 min
Calories p. portion: 180
2 portions
Allergens:

Quantity of ingredients
Rhubarb 5/8 oz / 200g. (recommended)
Apple juice (natural cloudy) 1 cup / 300g. (yes)
Corn starch 1 oz / 30g. (little)
Honey 1/2 oz / 20g. (yes)
Vanilla sugar natural 1 pinch / 0,5g. (yes)
Cinnamon ground 1 pinch / 0,5g. (yes)
Peppermint 2 leaves / 2g. (yes)

Cooking instructions:
Add the cornstarch to a 1/2 cup apple juice.
Simmer the rhubarb in 1 cup of water for 10 min.
Add the remaining apple juice and the cornstarch, stir, heat till it boils again.
Sweet with honey and season with vanilla and cinnamon. Spread the mixture on dessert bowls and garnish with mint.

9.62 Rice congee with honey pear and black sesame

Promotes digestion, supports urination, good to fight blood circulation disorders, thromboses, risk of embolism, high blood pressure, a headache, heart attack and stroke.
Cooking time approx. 10 min - 3 hours
Calories p. portion: 158
2 portions
Allergens: N

Quantity of ingredients
Basic recipe for a rice soup (Congee) 1 1/2 cups / 240g. (yes)
Pear 2 pieces / 300g. (recommended)
Sesame, black 1 teaspoon / 3g. (yes)

Cooking instructions:
Cook rice congee according to basic recipe.
Fill pot with 3 cm of water and heat till it boils. Quarter the pears (with the skin and seeds) and simmer them covered with black sesame for 10 minutes. Mix with the rice.

9.63 Rice with parsnips

Rich in vitamins, minerals potassium and zinc. Good to fight blood circulation disorders, thrombose, risk of embolism, high blood pressure, a headache, heart attack and stroke, yeast infections.
Cooking time approx. 45 min
Calories p. portion: 206
3 portions
Allergens:

Quantity of ingredients
Rice variety any 1 cup / 120g. (yes)
Water 1 1/2 cups / 200g. (yes)
Salt 1 pinch / 1g. (little)
Parsnip 3-4 pieces / 450g. (yes)
Olive oil 1 table spoon / 10g. (yes)
Sage 1 teaspoon / 3g. (yes)

Cooking instructions:
Peel the parsnips and cut into slices. Fry for a short time in oil. Add the rice and fry again for a short time. Add the water and cook it at least 30 min. Sprinkle with fresh chopped sage.

9.64 Ricepudding

Regulates gastrointestinal function. Strengthens spleen and stomach, strengthens the muscles. Vitamin C rich.
Cooking time approx. 2 hours and more
Calories p. portion: 316
1 portions
Allergens: G

Quantity of ingredients
Cow's milk (whole milk 3.5% fat) 3/4 cup - 6 oz / 200g. (yes)
Rice round grain 1 oz / 25g. (recommended)
Banana 1/4 lbs - 4oz / 100g. (yes)
Red berry (without sugar) 2 teaspoons / 4g. (yes)

Cooking instructions:
Heat half of the milk till it boils in a small saucepan.
Sprinkle the rice and cook on low heat for about 15 minutes.
Peel the banana, finely grate with the blender and add the beetroot juice.
Mix the banana bran under the hot rice.
Pour a pudding mold (about 1/4 liter of contents) in cold water.
Fill the banana rice in the mold and let the pudding swell at room temperature.
After about 3 hours it is solid and can be toppled.
Take the remaining milk as a drink.

9.65 Rosemary Potatoes

Reduces Inflammation, improves digestion, regenerates skin, supports urination, lowers cholesterol. Rosemary stimulates digestion, strengthens lung, promotes spleen and kidney, dries out.
Cooking time approx. 30 min
Calories p. portion: 188
2 portions
Allergens:

Quantity of ingredients
Potato 6-8 pieces / 420g. (yes)
Salt (herbal) 1 pinch / 1g. (yes)
Olive oil 1 table spoon / 10g. (yes)
Rosemary 1 teaspoon / 2g. (yes)

Cooking instructions:
Cut the potatoes into half´s, apply a little olive oil on the cut surface, then salt, sprinkle 2 - 3 rosemary needles on the potatoes.
Place the potatoes on the baking tray and bake them in the preheated oven for approx. 25 minutes to 190°C/374°F.

9.66 Salmon on tomato-spinach

Promotes bowel movement, improves blood circulation, forcing spleen and bowel, strengthens blood, reduces inflammation, improves digestion, regenerates skin, supports urination, lowers cholesterol, promotes sweating, dissolves stagnation.
Cooking time approx. 1 hour
Calories p. portion: 365
6 portions
Allergens: D

Quantity of ingredients
Potato 1,1 lbs / 500g. (yes)
Salt 1 pinch / 1g. (little)
Salmon 1,3 lbs / 600g. (recommended)
Rapeseed oil 2 teaspoons / 24g. (recommended)
Tomato 1/4 lbs - 4oz / 100g. (recommended)
Spinach 1,5 lbs / 700g. (yes)
Salt 1 pinch / 1g. (little)
Pine nuts 4 table spoons / 40g. (yes)
Leek 1/4 lbs - 4oz / 120g. (yes)
Olive oil 4 table spoons / 40g. (yes)
Salt 1 pinch / 1g. (little)
Pepper white (ground) 1 pinch / 0,5g. (yes)

Cooking instructions:
Peel the potato and cut into cubes, cook in salted water.
Cut the salmon into portions and fry slowly and evenly in a frying pan
from both sides, seasoned with salt and pepper, then add the pine nuts
and lightly roast.
Blanch spinach in salted water.
Lightly sweat the finely chopped leek with a little rapeseed oil, add the
blanched spinach and heat evenly.
Just before serving, add the halved cocktail tomatoes to the spinach
and season the vegetables well with salt and pepper.
Arrange the spinach and leek tomato bed with the potatoes, add the
salmon and sprinkle with the salted pine nuts.

Drizzle with a little olive oil and serve the dish.

9.67 Scrambled eggs with leaf salad olives and tomatoes

Calms nerves and stomach, relieves fatigue, regulates gastrointestinal
function, promotes digestion, stimulates liver function, detoxifying, helps
to digest fat, supports urination, reduces blood pressure.
Cooking time approx. 10 min
Calories p. portion: 419
1 portions
Allergens: C

Quantity of ingredients
Chicken egg 2-3 pieces / 180g. (yes)
Olive oil 1 table spoon / 10g. (yes)
Salt 1 pinch / 1g. (little)
Pepper (ground) 1 pinch / 0,5g. (yes)
Olives 6 pieces / 10g. (yes)
Tomato 1 piece / 50g. (recommended)
Lettuce 2 leaves / 5g. (recommended)
Turmeric (yellow root) 1 pinch / 1g. (yes)
Parsley 1/2 teaspoon / 5g. (yes)
Basil (fresh) 2-3 leaves / 2g. (yes)

Cooking instructions:
Heat olive oil in the pan. Cut the tomato into a slice. Pluck salad into small pieces. Briefly fry tomatoes, lettuce and olives. Meanwhile mix eggs with salt and spices with a fork.
Pour the egg and spices into the pan. Stir with a wooden spoon until it reaches the desired consistency.
Spices and herbs: turmeric, parsley, basil, black cumin
Variation: zucchini, rocket

9.68 Sliced chicken with walnuts and sherry

Strengthens blood, strengthens bone marrow, strengthens gastrointestinal function, expands blood vessels, prevents cancer, promotes perspiration, reduces blood lipids, stimulates.
Cooking time approx. 25 min
Calories p. portion: 304
4 portions
Allergens: EGHN

Quantity of ingredients
Butter organic 2 table spoons / 35g. (yes)
Walnuts 2 table spoons / 25g. (recommended)
Ginger fresh 1/2 teaspoon / 2g. (yes)
Onion (shallot) 2 pieces / 40g. (yes)
Salt 1 pinch / 1g. (little)
Chicken meat 3/4 lbs / 300g. (yes)
Peppers powder 1 pinch / 1g. (yes)
Sesame, white 1 teaspoon / 2g. (little)
Black fungus mushroom 4 pieces / 3g. (yes)
Shiitake, dried 4 pieces / 5g. (yes)
Soy sauce 1 dash / 3g. (yes)

Rice (whole grain) 1 cup / 120g. (yes)
Water 6 cups / 550g. (yes)
Salt 1 pinch / 1g. (little)

Cooking instructions:
Heat butter or sesame oil in a hot pan; Sauté walnuts, copious grated ginger, chopped shallots or onions; Add the salt and the sliced chicken and sauté everything; Rose paprika, roasted sesame, soaked black fungus, shiitake mushrooms or mushrooms; with a shot sherry; infuse with water; Simmer for 5 to 10 minutes until the meat is cooked; Season with soy sauce.

Place the rice in salted water, heat till it boils and let it simmer over low heat for about 15 minutes.

This fits: lamb's lettuce, Radicchio

9.69 Spicy avocado cream with cottage cheese

Anti-inflammatory, good to fight swelling, pain and itching, forcing spleen and digestive system, detoxifying, bactericide.
Cooking time approx. 15 min
Calories p. portion: 614
4 portions
Allergens: G

Quantity of ingredients
Avocado 2 pieces / 600g. (yes)
Pepper (ground) 1 pinch / 0,5g. (yes)
Salt 1 pinch / 1g. (little)
Lemon juice 1/2 piece / 15g. (yes)
Peppers powder 1 pinch / 1g. (yes)
Olive oil 1 table spoon / 10g. (yes)
Herbs various 1 table spoon / 7g. (yes)
Cottage cheese 1 cup / 250g. (yes)
Bread with carob kernel flour 8 slices / 200g. (recommended)

Cooking instructions:
Peel, core and purée avocados; add plenty of ground pepper, salt, lemon juice, rose paprika, a few drops of oil, chili, fresh chopped herbs, a pinch of salt; cottage cheese (about the same amount as avocado cream), carefully submerge.

Goes well with: Potatoes and millet, with which the avocado cream in combination with vegetable dishes, legumes or lettuce leaves a delicious meal. It is also very good as an appetizer, as a souvenir at parties and as a morning meal in the summer together with a mild dish of lentils or Adzuki beans and grated radish.

9.70 Spicy Tofu Vegetable Pan

Forcing spleen, relieves constipation, detoxifying, reduces inflammation, improves blood circulation, promotes sweating, dissolves stagnation, reduces flatulence, reduces blood pressure, strengthens immune system, prevents cancer, reduces radiation damage.
Cooking time approx. 25 min
Calories p. portion: 241
4 portions
Allergens: EN

Quantity of ingredients
Sesame oil 2 table spoons / 20g. (recommended)
Carrot 2 pieces / 100g. (recommended)
Fennel 1 piece / 250g. (recommended)
Leek 1 piece / 200g. (yes)
Salt 1 pinch / 1g. (little)
Turmeric (yellow root) 1 pinch / 1g. (yes)
Lemon juice 1 dash / 1g. (yes)
Soy Tofu 1 package / 120g. (yes)
Pepper (ground) 1 pinch / 0,5g. (yes)
Soy sauce 1 dash / 3g. (yes)
Rice (whole grain) 1 cup / 120g. (yes)
Water 6 cups / 500g. (yes)
Salt 1 pinch / 1g. (little)

Cooking instructions:
Heat sesame oil in a hot wok or a hot pan; fry the chopped carrots, fennel and leek slices; salt, a dash of lemon juice, turmeric, tofu cubes roast for 1 - 2 minutes.
Add the pepper and cook covered for about 5 minutes; drizzle with soy sauce.
Place the rice in salted water, heat till it boils and let it simmer over low heat for about 15 minutes.

9.71 Strawberry yoghurt and almond puree mix

Relieves pain and inflammation in rheumatism. Good to fight acute or chronic constipation of the intestine. Little laxative. Relieves pain, detoxifying, bactericide.
Cooking time approx. 5 min
Calories p. portion: 134
3 portions
Allergens: GH

Quantity of ingredients
Yogurt (natural, 1.5% fat) 5/8 oz / 200g. (recommended)
Strawberries 1,5 lbs / 700g. (recommended)
Honey 1 teaspoon / 3g. (yes)
Acerola fruit nectar or powder 1 teaspoon / 2g. (yes)
Almond puree 2 teaspoons / 6g. (yes)

Cooking instructions:
Puree yoghurt, strawberries, acerola, honey and almond paste in a blender.

9.72 Tea Black tea (Russian tea)

Black tea improves blood circulation.
Cooking time approx. 10 min
Calories p. portion: 7
1 portions
Allergens:

Quantity of ingredients
Black tea 1 table spoon / 5g. (yes)
Water 1 cup / 120g. (yes)

Cooking instructions:
For each cup you use a teaspoonful or a teabag.
Pour green tea only with 60 to 80 ° C / 140 to 176 °F hot water, otherwise it will be bitter.
If the tea has a stimulating effect, let it draw for two to three minutes. It has a calming effect for a duration of five minutes (no longer, otherwise it will be bitter!).
Another method: Pour the tea leaves with about 70 ° C / 158 °F hot water and pour the water immediately again.
Then just pour hot water again. The bitter substances disappear and the tea gets a milder aroma.

9.73 Tea Green tea

Green tea promotes digestion, supports urination, dissolves mucus, detoxifying, stimulates nerves, reduces blood lipids, lowers cholesterol, reduces inflammation.
Cooking time approx. 10 min
Calories p. portion: 2
1 portions
Allergens:

Quantity of ingredients
Green tea 1 teaspoon / 2g. (yes)
Water 1 cup / 120g. (yes)

Cooking instructions:
For each cup you use a teaspoonful or a teabag.
Pour green tea only with 60 to 80 ° C / 140 to 176 °F hot water, otherwise it will be bitter.
If the tea has a stimulating effect, let it draw for two to three minutes. It has a calming effect for a duration of five minutes (no longer, otherwise it will be bitter!).
Another method: Pour the tea leaves with about 70 ° C / 158 °F hot water and pour the water immediately again.
Then just pour hot water again. The bitter substances disappear and the tea gets a milder aroma.

9.74 Tomato soup

Promotes digestion, helps to digest fat, supports urination, reduces blood pressure, dissolves stagnation. Contains unsaturated fatty acids, is antioxidativ.
Cooking time approx. 10 min
Calories p. portion: 100
2 portions
Allergens:

Quantity of ingredients
Olive oil 1 table spoon / 15g. (yes)
Onion white 1 piece / 60g. (yes)
Basil (fresh) 1 teaspoon / 2g. (yes)
Cinnamon ground 1 pinch / 1g. (yes)
Pepper (ground) 1 pinch / 0,5g. (yes)
Salt 1 pinch / 1g. (little)
Tomato 6 pieces / 250g. (recommended)

Water 5/8 lbs - 8oz / 250g. (yes)
Peppers powder 1 pinch / 1g. (yes)

Cooking instructions:
Roast the onion in a pot. Salt and spices. Briefly roast. Put washed and quartered tomatoes in the pan. Stir and sauté briefly. Add a quart of water and heat till it boils. Cook for a quarter of an hour and puree.

9.75 Tonic Water

Chinin: Good to fight malaria.
Cooking time approx. 1 min
Calories p. portion: 95
1 portions
Allergens:

Quantity of ingredients
Tonic Water 1 cup / 250g. (yes)

Cooking instructions:
Buy tonic water and drink in small sips. A nice glass also increases your appetite.

9.76 Vanilla cream with berries

Weakness, chronic constipation of the intestine, weight loss, laxative, detoxifying, blood detoxifying. Strengthens the defense. Good to fight fungi infections.
Cooking time approx. 15 min
Calories p. portion: 278
4 portions
Allergens: G

Quantity of ingredients
Curd cheese 20% 7/8 lbs / 400g. (recommended)
Yogurt (natural, 1.5% fat) 3/8 lbs - 6oz / 150g. (recommended)
Sugar brown 2 teaspoons / 8g. (little)
Acerola fruit nectar or powder 1 teaspoon / 2g. (yes)
Vanilla sugar natural 3 package / 3g. (yes)
Cream (30% fat) 1/4 lbs - 4oz / 125g. (little)
Strawberries 1/4 lbs - 4oz / 100g. (recommended)
Raspberry 1/4 lbs - 4oz / 100g. (recommended)

Blackberry´s 1/4 lbs - 4oz / 100g. (recommended)
Blueberry 1/4 lbs - 4oz / 100g. (yes)

Cooking instructions:
Mix the curd cheese, yoghurt, sugar, acerola and vanilla sugar with a
hand mixer or whisk until smooth. Beat the whipped cream very stiff,
mix it under the cream. Arrange vanilla cream in portions with the
berries.

9.77 Vanilla pudding

Helps to fight constipation.
Cooking time approx. 10 min
Calories p. portion: 254
2 portions
Allergens: G

Quantity of ingredients
Cow's milk (whole milk 3.5% fat) 2 cups / 500g. (yes)
Pudding powder vanilla 1 package / 37g. (yes)
Sugar white 1 table spoon / 12g. (little)

Cooking instructions:
Give 3-5 tablespoons of milk into a cup, bring the rest in a pot to boil.
Pour the powdered pudding into the cup and stir until free of lumpy. As
soon as the milk boils, add the mixture and simmer under low heat for
about 3 minutes.
Divide into prepared bowls.

9.78 Vegetable juice

Promotes digestion, helps to digest fat, supports urination, reduces
blood pressure, strengthens immune system, prevents cancer, reduces
radiation damage, forcing spleen, is stimulating.
Cooking time approx. 15 min
Calories p. portion: 64
1 portions
Allergens: L

Quantity of ingredients
Celery root 1/2 oz / 20g. (recommended)
Carrot 1/4 lbs - 4oz / 100g. (recommended)
Tomato 1/4 lbs - 4oz / 100g. (recommended)
Garlic 1 piece / 2g. (yes)
Salt 1 teaspoon / 2g. (little)
Acerola fruit nectar or powder 1/2 teaspoon / 1g. (yes)

Cooking instructions:
Peel all ingredients and use the juicer to make a drink. Stir in the acerola.

9.79 Vegetable miso soup with tofu

Very powerful, strengthens after febrile illness, reduces blood pressure, strengthens immune system, prevents cancer, reduces radiation damage, improves blood circulation, strengthens liver and kidney, detoxifying, strengthens the muscles, reduces flatulence, forcing spleen.
Cooking time approx. 15 min
Calories p. portion: 107
4 portions
Allergens: EN

Quantity of ingredients
Sesame oil 2 table spoons / 35g. (recommended)
Onion (shallot) 1 piece / 20g. (yes)
Carrot 1 piece / 70g. (recommended)
Leek 2 inches / 10g. (yes)
Water 3 cups / 750g. (yes)
Endive salad 2 table spoons / 30g. (yes)
Soy Tofu 2 table spoons / 30g. (yes)
Ginger fresh 1/2 teaspoon / 1g. (yes)
Miso 2 table spoons / 15g. (yes)

Cooking instructions:
In sesame oil first sauté onions, then carrots and a little leek; Pour in water and simmer gently; add the bean sprouts and endive leaves and leave to stand; Tofu cubes, add a little ginger; at the end stir in a little cooled cooking-water the Miso.

9.80 Vegetable rice

Forcing spleen, dissolves stagnation, promotes weight loss. Good to fight immunodeficiency, loss of appetite, flatulence, high blood pressure, strengthens kidney and bladder. Diuretic, warming the body from the inside, regulates internal organs functions.
Cooking time approx. 30 min
Calories p. portion: 304
3 portions
Allergens: L

Quantity of ingredients
Broccoli 1/8 lbs - 2oz / 50g. (recommended)
Carrot 1/8 lbs - 2oz / 50g. (recommended)
Kohlrabi 1/8 lbs - 2oz / 50g. (recommended)
Cauliflower 1 oz / 30g. (recommended)
Peas 1/2 oz / 20g. (yes)
Margarine 1 teaspoon / 4g. (yes)
Rice (whole grain) 5/8 oz / 200g. (yes)
Basic recipe for a vegetable soup (nutritious) 7/8 lbs / 400g. (yes)
Parsley 1/2 oz / 20g. (yes)
Pepper (ground) 1 pinch / 0,2g. (yes)

Cooking instructions:
Cut the broccoli, carrots and kohlrabi into small cubes, divide the cauliflower into small florets. Heat the margarine in a pan or saucepan, sauté the vegetables. Then add the rice, top up with the vegetable stock and leave to soak for 15-20 minutes.

In the meantime finely chop the parsley. After cooking, season the rice with freshly ground pepper and parsley.

9.81 Vitamin drink

Regulates gastrointestinal function, promotes spleen and liver, reduces blood pressure, strengthens immune system, prevents cancer, reduces radiation damage, supports urination, quenches thirst, calms the stomach, prevents cancer.
Cooking time approx. 5 min
Calories p. portion: 172
3 portions
Allergens:

Quantity of ingredients
Orange juice 1 cup / 300g. (yes)
Carrot 5/8 oz / 200g. (recommended)
Banana 2 pieces / 300g. (yes)
Kiwi 1 piece / 20g. (yes)

Cooking instructions:
Chop oranges, carrots, bananas and kiwi and finely puree with the blender.

9.82 Warming carrot soup

Strengthens and warms, reduces blood pressure, strengthens immune system, prevents cancer, reduces radiation damage, strengthens gastrointestinal function.
Cooking time approx. 30 min
Calories p. portion: 133
3 portions
Allergens: HL

Quantity of ingredients
Carrot 4 pieces / 250g. (recommended)
Walnut oil 2 table spoons / 20g. (yes)
Onion (shallot) 2 pieces / 40g. (yes)
Anise (Common Fennel) 1/2 teaspoon / 1g. (yes)
Nutmeg 1 pinch / 1g. (yes)
Ginger fresh 1/2 teaspoon / 1g. (yes)
Salt 1 pinch / 1g. (little)
Basic recipe for a vegetable soup (nutritious) 2 cup / 500g. (yes)
Parsley 1 table spoon / 10g. (yes)

Cooking instructions:
Heat walnut oil in a hot pot and fry onions; steam the carrots in it; add anise, nutmeg, a little ginger, salt and sauté everything; add water or vegetable- or meat stock; cook everything soft and then puree; fold in parsley at the end.

Recommendation: Suitable for the cold season, especially if you use meat broth as a liquid for infusion.

9.83 Wild garlic pesto

Improves the flow characteristics of the blood, high vitamin C content, stomach- und blood detoxifying, good to fight arteriosclerosis, high blood pressure.
Cooking time approx. 10 min
Calories p. portion: 796
2 portions
Allergens: G

Quantity of ingredients
Wild garlic (garlic spinach) 1/4 lbs - 4oz / 125g. (yes)
Parmesan 1 oz / 30g. (yes)
Pine nuts 1/8 lbs - 2oz / 50g. (yes)
Olive oil 1/4 lbs - 4oz / 125g. (yes)
Salt 1 pinch / 1g. (little)
Pepper (ground) 1 pinch / 0,3g. (yes)

Cooking instructions:
Fresh wild garlic: Wash the wild garlic leaves and dry them carefully. Cut the wild garlic leaves into fine strips.
Dried wild garlic: Leave approx. 80g in 40g of water for 10 minutes.
Carefully roast the pine nuts. The pine nuts should be light brown after roasting. Cut the pine nuts very finely with a large knife or rub them with a nut mill. Pick up some of the seeds to decorate the pesto later.
Place all ingredients in a tall container and chop and mix with a blender.
Put the pesto in a bowl or in a glass.
In the fridge, the pesto lasts a while (days to weeks) and is therefore a way to preserve bear's garlic.
You can eat wild garlic pesto as sauce with spaghetti, but it also tastes great with potatoes or bread.

9.84 Yogurt with honey and nuts

Relieves pain, detoxifying, promotes wound healing. Good to fight acute or chronic constipation of the intestine. Dissolves stones.
Cooking time approx. 5 min
Calories p. portion: 258
1 portions
Allergens: GH

Quantity of ingredients
Yogurt (natural, 3.5% fat) 1/4 lbs - 4oz / 125g. (yes)
Honey 2 table spoons / 30g. (yes)

Walnuts 1 table spoon / 12g. (recommended)

Cooking instructions:
Mix yoghurt with honey and finely chopped nuts.

10 Effects of food

10.1 Use ingredients: recommendable

Acai powder
Apple (sour)
Apple (sweet)
Apple puree
Asparagus (green or white)
Beans (green, fresh)
Bitter Herb liqueur
Blackberry´s
Borage
Bread with carob kernel flour
Broccoli
Brussels sprouts
Carrot
Carrot (Early Carrot)
Carrot juice without sugar
Cauliflower
Celery root
Celery sticks
Cherry
Cherry (sour)
Chicory
Chinese cabbage
Cod
Corn germ oil
Cranberry
Cranberry juice
Cream 10% coffee cream
Cucumber
Cucumber (bitter)
Cucumber (spicy cucumber)
Curd cheese 20%
Currant (black)
Currant (red)
Currant (white)
Fennel
Fish pieces mixed (fresh water)
Fox nut, gorgon nut, makhana
Gourd
Herbal tea mix
Herring
Hibiscus
Juniper berry

Kohlrabi
Kudzu
Lamb's lettuce
Lamb's lettuce
Leaf salads (bitter)
Lentils
Lettuce
Lily bulbs
Linseed oil
Mackerel
Mascarpone cheese
Mediterranean fish (cod, plaice,
haddock, sea eel, mackerel)
Muesli
Peaches
Peaches (canned)
Pear
Peppers
Plaice
Plum
Plums
Processed cheese 12%
Radicchio
Radish
Radish (white, green, purple-red)
Radish horseradish
Rapeseed oil
Raspberry
Red beet
Red cabbage
Rhubarb
Rice long grain rice
Rice mash
Rice round grain
Rice sticky
Rose hip
Rose hip tea
Rosefish
Rucola
Salmon
Savory
Savoy cabbage / kale

Sesame oil
Soya Cuisine (soy cream)
Soybeans
Strawberries
Tomato
Trout
Tuna
Turkey breast meat
Turnip
Turnips

Vegetable juice
Walnuts
Watermelon
Wax gourd
Wheat germ oil
White cabbage
Wild herbs
Yogurt (natural, 1.5% fat)
Zucchini

10.2 Use ingredients: yes

Acerola fruit nectar or powder
Adzuki beans
Agar agar (kelp)
Agave nectar
Agrimony
Almond
Almond marzipan
Almond milk
Almond puree
Aloe juice
Amaranth
Amaranth Pops
Anchovy / Sardine
Angelica root
Anise (Common Fennel)
Apple juice (natural cloudy)
Apricot
Apricot dried
Apricot jam
Apricot nectar
Apricots
Apricots juice
Arrowroot
Artichoke
Aubergine
Avocado
Baking powder
Balm
Bamboo shoots
Banana
Banana (cooking banana)
Banchatee (green tea)
barberry
Barley grass powder
Barley malt
Basic recipe for a beef soup
Basic recipe for a beef soup (warming)
Basic recipe for a chicken soup
(warming)
Basic recipe for a duck soup
Basic recipe for a fish soup

Basic recipe for a rice soup (Congee)
Basic recipe for a vegetable soup
(nutritious)
Basil
Basil (fresh)
Batavia
Bay leaf
Bean oil
Bearberry leaf
Beef bone marrow
Beef fillet
Beef heart
Beef heart (calf)
Beef lungs (calf)
Beef meat
Beef meat (calf)
Beef meatbones
Beef Oxtail pieces
Beef soup meat
Beef stomach
Berries of the season
Berry juice
Bitter Lemon
Bitter orange peel
Black beans
Black caraway
Black fungus mushroom
Black tea
Blackberry dried (unripe fruit)
Blackberry jam
Blackberry leaves
Black-eyed peas
Blackthorn (Sloe)
Blue mallow tee
Blueberry
Blueberry dried
Blueberry jam
Blueberry juice
Bocksdorn fruits (Fructus Lycii, Goji,
goji berry dried
Boletus mushroom

Borage oil
Boxhorn clover seeds
Brazil nuts
Brie cheese
Broad beans (thick beans)
Buckbean
Buckwheat
Buckwheat (roasted) Kasha
Burdock root tea
Bush beans
Butter (half fat)
Butter beans white
Butter organic
Buttermilk
Calamari
Camembert
Cantaloupe
Capers in olive oil
Carambola (Star fruit)
Cardamom
Carob flour, St. john's bread
Carp
Cashews
Caviar
Cereal coffee
Chamomile
Chamomile tea
Champignon
Channa-Dal
Chanterelle
Chard
Chenpi (chinese tangerine bowl)
Cherry compote
Cherry juice
Chervil
Chervil dried
Chestnut puree
Chestnuts
Chicken Blood
Chicken egg
Chicken egg white
Chicken heart
Chicken meat
Chicken stomach
Chickpeas
Chickweed
Chili (pod or ground)
Chinese pearl barley
Chives
Chlorella (fresh water)
Chrysanthemum blossom tea
Cinnamon ground
Cinnamon sticks
Clementine

Clementines
Clove
Cocoa
Coconut flakes
Coconut grated
Coconut meat
Coconut milk
Codfish
Coffee
Coix (seeds) YiYi Ren
Cola drink (low calorie)
Compote (fruits of the season)
Cooking oil
Coriander
Coriander (fresh)
Corn silk tea
Cottage cheese
Cow's milk (1.5% fat)
Cow's milk (whole milk 3.5% fat)
Crab
Cranberries
Cranberry
Cranberry jam
Cream sour 10%
Cream sour 20%
Cream sour 30%
Creamer
Créme fraiche cheese
Cress
Crucian
Cumin (Caraway seed)
Curcuma
Curd cheese 40%
Currant jam (black)
Currant jam (red)
Currant juice (black)
Currants (black)
Currants (red)
Curry
Curry paste red
Daisy
Dandelion (young plants)
Dandelion juice
Dandelionroots tea
Dashi
Dates dried
Dates red
Deer meat
Deer meat
Deer's Bones
Deer's kidneys
Dill
Duck (heart)
Duck (slaughtered)

Ducks egg
Dulse (seaweed)
Dyer's broom herb
Edam cheese
Eel
Eel smoked
Elderberries
Elderberry blossom tee
Emmental cheese
Endive salad
Evening primrose oil
Fennel seeds ground
Fennel tea
Fenugreek (Trigonella foenum-graecum)
Feta cheese
Feta cheese
Fig
Fig dried
Fish sauce
Flounder
Flower pollen
French beans
Fresh cheese
Fresh cheese from soya
Fresh cheese with herbs
Freshwater crab
Freshwater fish
Fructose (glucose)
Fruit mix juice
Fruit tea
Gail plum
Galangal
Garam Masala powder
Garlic
Gelatin white
Gelee Royal
Gentian root
Gentian root tea
Ginger fresh
Ginger oil
Ginger powder
Ginkgo fruit
Ginseng
Ginseng root
Goat
Goat and sheep's blood
Goat and sheep's brain
Goat and sheep's milk
Goat and sheep's stomach
Goat cheese
Goose
Goose blood
Goose egg

Goose fat
Goose parts
Gooseberry
Gorgonzola
Gouda cheese
Grape juice red
Grape juice white
Grapefruit (Pomelo)
Grapefruit dried peel
Grapefruit juice
Grapes red
Grapes white
Grapeseed oil
Grass carp
Green tea
Greengage
Ground
Ground caraway
Guava
Halibut (Flatfish)
Hawthorn
Hazelnuts
Herbs bitter
Herbs of Provence
Herbs various
Herbs wild
Hibiscus tea
Hijiki
Hokkaido pumpkin
Honey
Hop
Horehound leaves
Horse meat
Hyssop
Iceberg lettuce
Jasmine blossoms tee
Jellyfish
Kaki plum
Kalmus
Kefir
Kidney beans (red)
King Solomon's-seal
Kiwi
Kombu seaweed (Saccharina japonica)
Kukicha tea
Kumquats
Ladyfingers
Lamb bones
Lamb meat
Lamb shoulder
Lavender blossoms
Leek
Lemon
Lemon Balm (dried)

Lemon Balm (fresh)
Lemon juice
Lemon peel
Lemongrass
Lentils black
Lentils red
Lentils yellow
Licorice root tea
Lima beans
Lime
Lime blossom tea
Liver smoothing tea
Lobster
Longane
Loquate / Japanese medlar
Lotus roots
Lotus seeds
Lovage
Lovage seeds
Luo Han Guo fruit
Lychee
Lychee in Preserved
Mallow (Malva sylvestris) blossom tea
Mango
Mango juice
Maple syrup
Mare's milk
Margarine
Margarine (diet)
Marjoram
Medlar
Mineral water
Mirabelle plum
Miso
Miso black (fermented)
Miso paste (soy bean paste)
Mixed Pickles
Mold cheese
Morel (black, dried)
Morel, dried
Mozzarella
Mu Erh Mushroom
Mulberry fruit
Mulled Wine Spice
Mullet
Mung bean
Mung bean sprouting
Mussels
Mustard
Mustard Dijon
Mustard medium hot
Mustard seeds
Mustard sweet
Mutton

Mutton
Nasturtium (nose-twister or nose-tweaker)
Nectarine
Nettles
Nori, purple seaweed, red algae
Nutmeg
Octopus
Octopus
Okra
Olive oil
Olives
Olives green
Onion (shallot)
Onion (spring onion)
Onion read
Onion white
Orange
Orange blossom
Orange dried peel
Orange grated peel
Orange jam
Orange juice
Orange peel
Oregano dried
Oregano fresh
Oyster mushroom
Oyster shell powder
Oysters
Palm oil
Papaya
Parmesan
Parsley
Parsley root
Parsnip
Passion blossoms tea
Passion fruit
Peanut butter
Peanut oil
Peanuts
Pear juice
Peas
Peas, green
Pepper (ground)
Pepper Cayenne
Pepper powder (hot)
Pepper white (ground)
Peppercorns
Peppermint
Peppermint tea
Pepperoni
Pepperoni, red, pitted, halved
Pepperoni, yellow, pitted, halved
Peppers (rose peppers)

Peppers (sweet)
Peppers powder
Perch
Pheasant
Pickle
Pig blood
Pigeon
Pigeon egg
Pimento
Pine nuts
Pineapple
Pineapple (from a can)
Pineapple juice without sugar
Pinto beans speckled
Pistachios
Plum dried
Pomegranate
Poppy
Pork Bacon
Pork brain
Pork fat (lard)
Pork ham
Pork ham cooked
Pork ham smoked
Pork knuckle
Pork lung
Pork marrow bones
Pork meat
Pork skin
Pork stomach
Pork/beef sausage (smoked)
Pork's intestine
Potato
Potato (mealy)
Potato flour
Prickly pear
processed cheese 30%
Psyllium seed
Pudding powder vanilla
Puff pastry
Pumpkin
Pumpkin seed oil
Pumpkin seeds
Quail
Quail egg
Quince
Quinoa
Rabbit
Rabbit (wild)
Rabbit liver
Rabbit meat
Radish black
Radish leaves
Raisins

Raspberry dried (immature)
Raspberry jam
Raspberry leaf tea
Red berry (without sugar)
Reishi mushroom
Ribworttea
Rice (fragrance)
Rice (Gaoliang / Sorghum)
Rice (whole grain)
Rice Basmati
Rice flour
Rice malt
Rice noodles
Rice red
Rice starch
Rice variety any
Rice wild (nature rice)
Romaine lettuce / lettuce salad
Rose blossom tea
Rose leaf tea
Rosemary
Safflower (Dyer's thistle / Hong Hua)
Saffron
Sage
Sake
Salsify
Salt (herbal)
Sauerkraut (cutted cabbage fermented)
Sea buckthorn
Sea cucumber
Seacrab
Sesame oil roasted
Sesame paste (Tahini)
Sesame, black
Shark
Sheep's milk
Sheep's milk yoghurt
Shiitake, dried
Shrimp
Shrimps
Skim milk powder
Slug
Sorrel
Sour cherries
Sour cream 15% fat
Sour milk
Sour milk cheese 20%
Soy flour
Soy noodles
Soy sauce
Soy Tofu
Soy Tofu smoked
Soybean milk
Soybean oil

Soybeans, black
Soybeans, blacks, fermented
Soybeans, yellow
Spinach
Spiny lobsters
Spurdog (spiny dogfish, Schillerlocken)
St. Benedict's thistle, blessed thistle,
holy thistle, spotted thistle
Star anise
Stevia (candyleaf, sweetleaf)
Strawberry jam
Strawberry Juice
Sugar fructose - fruit sugar
Sugar glucose - grapes sugar
Sugar Milk Sugar
Sugar substitute (sweetener)
Sunflower oil
Sunflower seeds
Sweet potato
Tabasco
Tangerine
Tarragon (Estragon)
Tea mixture uric acid lowering
Thistle oil
Thyme
Thyme dried
Tomato dried
Tomato juice
Tomato paste
Tomato puree
Tonic Water
Topinambur
Trout (smoked)
Truffle
Turkey ham

Turmeric (yellow root)
Umeboshi paste
Umeboshi plums (Japanese apricots)
Valerian
Vanilla
Vanilla pod
Vanilla powder
Vanilla sugar natural
Vinegar (Apple vinegar)
Vinegar (Red wine vinegar)
Vinegar Aceto Balsamico
Vinegar Aceto Balsamico white
Wakame
Walnut oil
Walnuts roasted
Water
Water hot
Wheat bulgur
Wheatgrass juice
Wheatgrass powder
Whey
White beans
Whitefish
Wild boar meat
Wild garlic (garlic spinach)
Wild strawberries
Wormwood herb
Yam root, yam root tuber
Yarrow
Yarrow tea
Yeast
Yew nut
Yoghurt vanilla
Yogi tea
Yogurt (natural, 3.5% fat)

10.3 Use ingredients: little

Beef kidney
Beef liver
Beer (alcohol-free)
Beer (alcohol-reduced)
Beer (Pils)
Beer (Top-fermented German dark
beer)
Bitter liqueur
Brown ale
Buckwheat whole grain
Campari
Chicken liver
Chicken yolk
Chocolate
Chocolate (Diabetic)

Clarified butter
Coconut fat
Cola drink
Corn flour
Corn starch
Cream (30% fat)
Cream, sweet 30%
Fernet Branca (herbal bitter liqueur)
Fish innards
Fish remains
Ginseng liqueur
Goat and sheep's liver
Green spelt
Honey wine (Met)
Lamb kidneys

Lamb liver
Linseed
Linseed (crushed)
Lychee liqueur
Martini
Mayonnaise 50%
Mayonnaise 80%
Peanut (roasted)
Pork heart
Pork kidneys
Pork Lard
Pork liver
Pork sausage (Bratwurst)
Prosecco
Red wine
Rice black
Rice sweet

Rum
Salt
Sesame, white
Sherry (whine)
Spirit
Sugar - icing sugar
Sugar brown
Sugar candy white
Sugar cane sugar
Sugar molasses
Sugar palm sugar
Sugar white
Tsampa (roasted barley flour)
Wheat beer
White wine
Wormwood

10.4 Do not use contra-acting foods

Barley
Barley flour
Barley grouts
Barley not peeled
Bread roll
Breadcrumbs (wheat bread, bread roll)
Bulgur (cereals)
Corn
Corn (fast polenta)
Corn (roasted)
Corn Grease (Polenta)
Couscous
Crispbread
Lye roll
Malt
Manioc flour
Millet
Millet flakes
Multi-grain bread (gray bread)
Noodles (wheat) with egg
Noodles (wheat, lasagne) with egg
Noodles (wheat, ribbon noodles) with egg
Noodles (wheat, spaghetti) with egg
Noodles (whole grain) with egg
Oat
Oat flakes (whole grain)
Oat flakes roasted
Oat flour
Oat fusion (baby food)
Oat meal
Oat milk
Pearl barley

Pearl barley
Pumpernickel (dark bread)
Rusk
Rye
Rye flour
Rye wholemeal bread
Sago (cereals)
Sourdough
Spelled (Dark) bread
Spelled flakes
Spelled grain
Spelled semolina
Spelled wholemeal flour
Supplementary nutrition
Toast bread (whole grain)
Wheat
Wheat bran
Wheat flakes
Wheat flatbread/pita bread
Wheat flour
Wheat flour whole grain
Wheat semolina
Wheat semolina for children
Wheat/Rye/Gray-black bread with yeast
White bread (baguette)
White bread (pretzel sticks)
White bread (roll)
White bread (wheat bread)
White breadcrumbs
White dumpling bread
Whole grain bread
Wholemeal flour

11 Herbs and their effects

11.1 Basil (fresh)

It has a beneficial effect on flatulence and nausea, relaxing and soothing. Good to fight emphysema, bronchitis, whooping cough, high blood pressure, headache, mouth odor, warts, hiccup, gout, migraine.

11.2 Mugwort

Reduces bleeding, alleviates pain. In the kitchen, mugwort is used as a spice for fat food. Since it contains many bitter substances, it boosts fat burning and promotes digestion.

11.3 Savory

Stomach-strengthening, soothing and appetizing. Ideal for prevent colds, strengthens the immune system. In case of incontinence or nocturnal wetting (not for children), put the beans in liquor for libido.

11.4 Nettles

Promotes urination. Tea or juice, cleanses the blood and the kidneys, supports prostate problems, inhibit the formation of inflammation, pain-relieving.

11.5 Dill

The medicinal and spice herb has an antispasmodic effect and stimulates gastric juice production. Good to fight flatulence. Antispasmodic for gastrointestinal discomfort.

11.6 Chamomile

Antispasmodic and anti-inflammatory for digestive disorders, soothes the nerves and promotes good sleep. Applied externally, it heals wounds in the mouth-throat area and the skin. Strengthens eyesight.

11.7 Chervil dried

Forces urination, detoxifying, blood-purifying and blood-pressure-reducing effects.

11.8 Coriander

The essential oils are appetizing, digestive, cramping and soothing in stomach and intestinal disorders.

11.9 Herbs various

Appetizing, lots of trace elements and vitamins

11.10 Cress

Diuretic, supports urination. Good to fight dry mouth, inner agitation, sore throat, diabetes, kidney stones, gastrointestinal complaints, lung problems, menstrual cramps or cancer.

11.11 Chives

Bactericide, prevents cancer, strengthens gastric juice production, promotes digestion and blood circulation, promotes growth, triggers stagnation.

11.12 Lovage

Stimulates digestion, reduces pain. Extracts of the root are used to flush out urinary tract infections and prevent kidney gravel.

11.13 Lily bulbs

Calms nerves, good to fight scaly skin. The onions and the petals are added to ointments in the Orient, which can heal muscles and tendons. White lily (astringent).

11.14 Dandelion (young plants)

Detoxifies, relieves inflammation. Regulates digestion, helps with rheumatism, releases kidney stones, leaves pimples and chronic skin disorders disappear.

11.15 Oregano dried

It has an anti-digestive, calming and nerve-strengthening effect, helps to fight cramping stomach and intestinal disorders. The ingredient Carvacrol has an anti-inflammatory effect.

11.16 Parsley

Stimulates liver function, detoxifies. Forces urinating. Relieves flatulence. Digestive and menstrual stimulating, birth-accelerating, memory-enhancing, blood-purifying, skin-smoothing.

11.17 Peppermint

Relaxes, frees the lungs and the nose (inhale), regulates the cycle. Stimulates bile flow and bile production, antispasmodic in gastrointestinal disorders, antimicrobial and antiviral.

11.18 Rosemary

Promotes digestion, relieves bloating, strengthens lung, spleen and kidney. Affects the circulation and nerves. Appetizing. Baths help to fight circulatory disorders as well as with gout and rheumatism.

11.19 Sage

Good to fight yeast infections. The leaves have a digestive effect and are used in greasy foods. Antiperspirant effect. Helps to relieve coughing attacks. Dries out (TCM).

11.20 Black caraway

Detoxifying, immunoregulatory. In addition, the oil should stimulate the formation of bone marrow cells and generally protect body cells from viruses.

11.21 Thyme dried

Disinfecting. It stimulates the blood circulation, increases the appetite and helps to digest fat meat better. Strengthens lungs and spleen (TCM).

11.22 King Solomon's-seal

Used to repair wounds or damaged tissue. Good to fight dry cough, earlier also tuberculosis and dysentery, as well as diarrhea and hemorrhoids.

11.23 Yam root, yam root tuber

Solves cramps (in the gastrointestinal tract). Digestive through increased bile production. Anti-inflammatory in rheumatic diseases. Mucolytic agent for coughing. Relief of menopausal symptoms.

11.24   Lemongrass

Reduction of flatulence, antimicrobial, appetizing. Prevention of influenza. Good to fight infections in the mouth and throat.

12 Basics of Nutrition

The basic principles of nutrition described herein are general recommendations. They are not aimed at a specific form of therapy. Recommendations concerning a therapy have priority.

12.1 Nutrition

Regular meals in a relaxed atmosphere. A warm breakfast is considered a good start into the day.
The main meals ought to be taken for lunch – supper in the early evening. Pay attention to feeling hungry or sated: don't eat too much nor remain hungry is the rule
Prepare the meals freshly from natural, regional products. Frozen, heat-conserved, industrially prepared or foodstuffs cooked in the microwave oven are rejected.
Choice of foodstuffs according to the season: more cooling food in summer, more warming food in winter.
Eat cooked food at least twice a day. Food and drinks ought to be lukewarm, never ice-cold or hot.
Raw vegetables, briefly cooked vegetables, freshly squeezed juices and mineral water are not recommended. Milk and dairy products are only included in the diet if they don't cause problems.
Don't use therapeutic recipes over a longer period without consulting your doctor or therapist.

Varied food
Enjoy the diversity of foodstuffs. Characteristics of a balanced nutrition are variety, suitable combination and a balanced quantity of rich and low energy foodstuffs (on one hand avoiding undersupply with essential nutrients and on the other hand to take to many undesirable substances).

A lot of Cereal Products - and Potatoes
Bread, pasta, rice, cereal flakes (best wholemeal) as well as potatoes contain almost no fat, but many vitamins, mineral nutrients, trace elements, roughage and secondary plant substances. These foodstuffs ought to be taken with low-fat side dishes.

Vegetables and Fruit – „Take Five" every day ...
5 portions of vegetables and fruit a day, as fresh as possible, briefly cooked, or maybe one portion as a juice – ideal as a side dish to every meal as well as snack between meals: Thus a lot of vitamins, mineral nutrients as well as roughage and secondary plant substances

Daily milk and dairy products
Milk and Dairy Products every Day, once or twice per Week Fish; meat, sausages as well as eggs moderately. These foodstuffs contain valuable nutrients like calcium in the milk, iodine selenium and omega-3 fat acids in saltwater fish. Meat is favorable due to its high content of disposable iron and the vitamins B1, B6 and B12. Quantities of 300 – 600 g meat and sausage per week are sufficient. Prefer low-fat products, especially in meat- and dairy products.

Low-fat and fatty Foodstuffs
Fat supplies us with essential fat acids and fatty foodstuffs contain also fat-soluble vitamins. Fat is high in energy; therefore much fat in the food may cause overweight, possibly also cancer. Too many saturated fat acids may further a tendency for cardio-vascular diseases in the long term. Prefer vegetable oils and fats (e.g. rapeseed-, olive-, soya-oils and solid fats produced therefrom). Beware of invisible fat in meat- and dairy products, pastry and sweets as well as in fast-food and convenience foods. 70 – 90 g fat per day is sufficient.

Moderately Sugar and Salt
Take sugar and foods/drinks containing various kinds of sugar (e.g. glucose syrup) only occasionally. Use herbs and spices as well as a little salt creatively. Prefer salt containing iodine.

Plenty of Liquids
Water is absolutely essential. Drink 1-2 l liquids every day. Prefer water (with or without gas) and other low-calorie drinks. Alcoholic drinks should not be taken.

Tasty Dishes, carefully cooked
Cook the meals with as low temperatures and as short as possible, using little water and fat – this preserves the original taste, keeps the nutrients intact and prevents the production of harmful compounds.

Take time and enjoy the food
Take your Time and enjoy your Food
Eating consciously helps to eat right. The eye enjoys food, too. It's fun, invites to enjoy varied dishes and stimulates the feeling of satiety.

Watch your Weight and stay in Motion
A balanced diet and a lot of exercise and sport (30 – 60 min/day) are a healthy combination. The right weight furthers well-being and health. Thermals, directional effectiveness, digestive power

There are various criteria for judging the effectiveness of herbs and foodstuffs.
The use of certain herbs and ingredients is based on observations of the effects on the body which these foodstuffs, herbs and spices show after having eaten them. The medical science has developed following system: Every ingredient or herb has a directional effectiveness. Furthermore, there are herbs which have a special effect on certain organs.
The basic condition for a healthy metabolism is to obtain sufficient energy from food and that the digestive process doesn't use too much energy. An easily digestible meal makes content and sated, doesn't cause flatulence and fatigue after the meal. The perfect spices increase the healthiness of our meals. Very often, just small doses of herbs and spices will suffice. They are not used to make us sated, but to help our digestive organs to digest the food.

12.2 Recipes

The recipes list the ingredients to be used and the cooking instructions show how the dish is prepared. The list of ingredients shows the concerned quantities as well as the relevance for the therapy. If you find „less than mentioned", try to comply or find an alternative from the „list of recommended foodstuffs". Mostly it shall result just in a small change of taste when you simply avoid this ingredient.
Mild cooking methods: boiling, stewing, poaching, steaming
Strong cooking methods: barbecuing, roasting, frying, smoking
Balanced cooking methods: deep-frying, baking brick
Deep-freezing and warming in the microwave oven should be avoided (denaturalization).

12.3 Foodstuffs

Foodstuffs have an effect on body and soul like medicinal herbs, only a very much milder one. Dietary advice is mainly based on regional foodstuffs. The knowledge about the effects of each foodstuff and the knowledge, when which foodstuff shall be used, is based on the orthodox school of medicine. Use ecologic-organic products, if possible. As everything should be cooked for a long time due to a better digestability and very rarely eaten raw, the food agrees with everyone.
The classification of the foodstuffs according to their effect on the body is the basis in order to achieve a harmonious status of health.

Dietary advisors do not recommend certain foodstuffs for everyone. The individual diet is tailor-made for the individual constitution.

Buy only fresh and ripe fruit and vegetables. You ought to leave unripe fruit and vegetables and such with brown spots and wilted leaves behind in the market. In this case take deep-frozen goods (never ready-to-serve dishes!). Fruit and vegetables are deep-frozen immediately after harvesting and often contain more vitamins and minerals than the goods from the vegetable shelf. Whereas conserved or tinned goods contain very much less biological substances. Also, salt, sugar and others are mostly added to the latter. Never leave the foodstuffs in the water after washing them to avoid that many vital substances get drowned. Clean salads, fruit and vegetables immediately before serving.

Please make sure of the hygienic processing of foodstuffs. Clean your salads, fruit and vegetables carefully. When cooking with meat, prepare all ingredients first and then process the meat products. Clean the worktop and tools very carefully. Wooden surfaces ought to be treated with a mild disinfectant regularly in order to reduce germination.

Store fruit and vegetables separately, if possible. Harvested fruit and vegetables are still alive and emit e.g. ethylene gas, which makes other products ripen and age faster. Keep meat and fish in the closed packaging or store them in the fridge in closed containers.

12.4 Herbs

There are some basic rules for storing medicinal herbs. On principle, herbs must be protected from direct sunlight, humidity and heat.

Containers for the storage of herbs may be glasses, ceramic jars and even plastic containers. However, plastic is a rather unsuitable material and should only be a short-term solution. In case of glass containers, use a dark material.

Medicinal herbs cannot be kept for any long period. The shelf life of herbs is limited. However, it can be prolonged with suitable storage. The place should be dark, rather cool and absolutely dry. A wooden medicine cabinet, placed not directly next to a source of heat, would be ideal. Never buy large quantities of herbs so as not to have to throw them away. Label the container with the name of the herb and the date of harvesting or processing.

13 Other dietic-books

The following syndromes of dietetics, TCM or for a therapy supplement for cancer are available.

Dietetics

E001. Nutrition of the infant - baby food
E002. Nutrition during lactation
E003. Nutrition in old age
E004. Nutrition of children and adolescents
E005. Nutrition of athletes
E006. Light weight
E007. Pregnancy
E008. Full food

Protein and electrolyte - kidneys
E009. (hemodialysis) dialysis treatment
E010. Acute renal failure
E011. Chronic renal insufficiency
E012. Nephrotic syndrome
E013. Kidney stones (nephrolithiasis)

Gastrointestinal tract - pancreas
E014. Acute pancreatitis (inflammation of the pancreas)
E015. Chronic pancreatitis (inflammation of the pancreas)

Gastrointestinal tract - small intestine and large intestine
E016. Acute obstipation (constipation)
E017. Chronic obstipation (constipation)
E018. Colon irritabile
E019. Diverticulitis
E020. Acquired lactose intolerance (lactose malabsorption)
E021. Fructose malabsorption
E022. Glutensensitive enteropathy (celiac disease)
E023. Colectomy
E024. Short Bowel Syndrome

Gastrointestinal tract - liver, gallbladder, bile ducts
E025. Acute and chronic hepatitis (inflammation of the liver)
E026. Cholelithiasis (bile stones)
E027. fatty liver
E028. cirrhosis

Gastrointestinal tract - Stomach and duodenal intestine
E029. Acute gastritis
E030. Chronic gastritis
E031. Stomach bleeding
E032. Ulcus ventriculi and duodenal ulcer
E033. Condition after gastric surgery

Gastrointestinal tract - oral cavity and esophagus
E034. Stomatitis
E035. Esophageal carcinoma (esophageal cancer)
E036. Refluosophagitis (heartburn)

Special diseases
E037. Phenylketonuria (PKU)
E038. Rheumatic joint diseases

Metabolism
E039. Obesity (overweight)
E040. Diabetes mellitus
E041. Eating disorders (underweight)

Fat metabolism
E042. Hypercholesterolaemia (increased cholesterol level)
E043. Hepatic Encephalopathy

Heart and circulation
E044. Arteriosclerosis (arterial calcification)
E045. Heart insufficiency
E046. Hypertension
E047. Hyperuricaemia and gout

Changed nutrient requirements
E048. In case of fever
E049. For malignant diseases
E050. After burns
E051. Radiation and chemotherapy

CANCER
E100. Pancreatic cancer
E101. Bladder cancer
E102. Blood cancer (leukemia)
E103. Breast cancer
E104. Colorectal cancer
E105. Gastric cancer
E106. Kidney cancer
E107. Esophageal cancer

TCM
E200. Bladder - moisture heat in the bladder
E201. Bladder - moisture and cold in the bladder
E202. Bladder - emptiness and cold in the bladder
E203. Large intestine - external cold affects the large intestine
E204. Large intestine - moisture heat in the large intestine
E205. Large intestine - heat blocks the intestine II acute
E206. Large intestine - dryness of the colon
E207. Large intestine - Yang deficiency (cold)
E208. Heart - Blood insufficiency
E209. Heart - Blood stagnation
E210. Heart - Fire
E211. Heart - Hot mucus clogs the heart pores

E212. Heart - Cold mucus clogs the heart pores
E213. Heart - Qi deficiency
E214. Heart - Yang deficiency
E215. Heart - Yin deficiency
E216. Liver - Ascending Liver Yang
E217. Liver - Blood deficiency
E218. Liver - Blood stagnation
E219. Liver - Moisture heat in liver and gall bladder
E220. Liver - Fire
E221. Liver - Gall bladder Qi-Empty
E222. Liver - Cold in the liver meridian
E223. Liver - Qi stagnation
E224. Liver - Wind
E225. Liver - Wind with ascending liver Yang
E226. Liver - Wind with blood anemic
E227. Liver - Wind with extreme heat
E228. Lung - Qi deficiency
E229. Lung - Mucus-moisture in the lungs
E230. Lung - Mucus-heat in the lungs
E231. Lung - Mucus-cold in the lungs
E232. Lung - Dryness of the lungs
E233. Lung - Wind-heat attacks the lungs
E234. Lung - Wind-cold affects the lungs
E235. Lung - Yin deficiency
E236. Stomach - Bloodstagnation
E237. Stomach - Fire
E238. Stomach - Cold with liquid
E239. Stomach - Nutrition stagnation
E240. Stomach - Qi deficiency
E241. Stomach - Rebellious Qi
E242. Stomach - Yin Emptiness
E243. Spleen - Heat and moisture attack the spleen
E244. Spleen - Coldness and moisture affects the spleen
E245. Spleen - Qi deficiency
E246. Spleen - Qi deficiency + Declining spleen Qi
E247. Spleen - Qi deficiency + spleen does not control the blood
E248. Spleen - Yang deficiency
E249. Kidney - Heart and kidney no longer communicate
E250. Kidney - Jing deficiency
E251. Kidney - Kidneys cannot receive the Qi
E252. Kidney - Qi is not stable
E253. Kidney - Yang deficiency
E254. Kidney - Yin deficiency

For further information visit di-book.com.